RICHARD WAGNER
Stories and Essays

RICHARD WAGNER
Stories and Essays

Selected, edited and introduced by

CHARLES OSBORNE

Distributed by
OPEN COURT
Publishing Co.
La Salle, Ill. 61301

800-435-6850   or   815-223-2521

ISBN: 0 912050-43-8
LCCCN: 72 13588

The items in this book were originally published in
German under the following titles: 'Ueber das Dichten
und Komponieren'; 'Das Judentum in der Musik'; 'Was
ist Deutsch?'; 'Eine Pilgerfahrt zu Beethoven'; 'Ein
glücklicher Abend'; 'Ein Ende in Paris'; 'Ueber das
Opern-Dichten und Komponieren im Besonderen'; 'Der
Virtüose und der Künstler'; 'Die Wibelungen'. They are
taken from *Die Gesammetten Schriften und Dichtungen
von Richard Wagner*.

First published in the United States of America
in 1973 by The Library Press, New York

This edition © Charles Osborne and Peter Owen Ltd 1973

Printed in Great Britain

Contents

Introductory Note

Wagner was both theorist and artist. For the most part a somewhat absurd theorist, he just happened as a composer to possess or be possessed by genius. He was fortunately not at the mercy of his own theories : it would be, although a simplification, by no means an untruth to say that his masterpieces exist despite these theories, not because of them. It must be admitted that, in several of his essays, Wagner's prose and his thought processes are both extremely impenetrable. The essays remain fascinating, however, for the light they shed on the composer. It is also unfortunately true that some of Wagner's theories, which he was venal enough to adopt and discard always at the expedient moment, are as conscienceless as his character : a character which allowed him to be callous in personal relationships, dishonest in business dealings, and unreliable in most other matters. But Wagner's theories, too, are obviously of interest to students of the composer. In any case, if you can write *Der fliegende Holländer* or *Tristan und Isolde*, you do not need character. (On the other hand, if you can write *Parsifal*, you are wanting in something which I would call artistic discretion.)

Wagner's famous theory of the music drama boils down to no more than an exhortation to the mid-nineteenth century to take opera as seriously as Handel, Gluck and Mozart had done. But the composer's vanity stood in the way of his heeding his own advice in this instance; for instead of collaborating with a dramatist of distinction, he preferred to write his own libretti. The results are frequently as clumsily illiterate as the work of the worst of the Italian hack librettists whom he derides, and are additionally burdened by Wagner's teutonic inability to be concise. The drama in Wagner's great operas is provided entirely by the music, which is often seriously hampered by the portentous autodidactic doggerel churned out by the composer-as-poet. That much of it is of

7

psychoanalytical interest has tended to obscure the fact that the libretto of, for instance, *Parsifal* is really very poor dramatic verse. The sad truth is that Wagner lacked any feeling for words as the raw material of art, though he possessed the artist's instinct as far as his own requirements were concerned. Wagner the composer needed Wagner the poet. He would not have been happy with, say, Goethe or Schiller.

The prose works of Wagner occupy ten volumes in the collected German edition; they appeared in English translation in eight volumes between 1892 and 1899. The longer essays, such as *Das Kunstwerk der Zukunft* (The Work of Art of the Future) and *Oper und Drama* (Opera and Drama), have since been published separately, and are reasonably accessible. For inclusion in this present volume I have selected several of the shorter, lesser-known essays, as well as the notorious *Judentum in der Musik* (Judaism in Music), and the naïvely charming short stories about an unsuccessful German composer, which Wagner first published in Paris. *Das Judentum in der Musik* is the only piece I have completely retranslated. For the others, I have used the W. Ashton Ellis translations of 1892-9 as a basis, amending where necessary for the sake of clarity. I have prefaced each piece with a few explanatory notes.

Charles Osborne

On Poetry and Composition

As *Über das Dichten und Komponieren*, this was published in the Bayreuth Festival Theatre's 'house' magazine, *Bayreuther Blätter*, in July 1879, and reprinted in Volume 10 of the second edition of the collected works in 1888.

*

Perhaps this should be called 'On the Book and Music Trade'. To some that may seem too frivolous a view of the matter. Yet the departed Gutzkow has divulged to us the awful secret that the unbounded popularity of Goethe and Schiller is simply due to the energetic speculation of their publishers. Though this explanation hardly applies nowadays, the fact that it was put forward at least shows that our writers consider it possible for their own publishers to achieve a similar success. By this method, it would take considerable capital to plant the German 'Poets' Corner'; accordingly we need not be surprised if the publisher considers he has played the major part in the production of poetic works, especially of such as aim at notoriety. Thus we may assume an odd relationship between poets and their publishers, in which mutual esteem plays but a small part. A famous poet once assured me that publishers were enabled to be the most knavish of dealers, because their dealings were exclusively with unworldly artists, whereas all other middlemen did business with people as cunning as themselves. At any rate, the case seems pretty bad To ensure renown, the poet or composer finds it best to seek the sponsorship of some huge firm of publishers. Such a

9

firm has to lay out a fortune at enormous establishments for printing or engraving. These must be always kept at work, with the result that the publisher is obliged to undertake the manufacture of a certain amount of useless stuff. Often, all the publicity in the world cannot help him to dispose of it. Occasionally, however, he hits on a remarkably fine work, the product of a unique intellect. With the success of this one work, the publisher recoups all his previous losses; and if the author wants to have his share of the profits, the publisher can coolly shake him off with the retort that he has borne no part in the expenses attending a perpetual output of rubbish. On the other hand, it is just this perpetual output that hoists the publisher to eminence. Everybody nowadays writes poetry or music, which the huge firm must constantly print and issue : the habit and the necessity complement each other. But the publisher has the advantage in that he can show his clients how much he loses and at the same time prove his generosity by declaring himself quite ready to proceed with further editions, thereby putting the imaginative author very much in his debt. Thus the book and music publisher, the poet and composer's employer, their populariser, may in certain cases, as alleged for Schiller and Goethe, be regarded with some reason as the patron saint, if not the creator, of our poetic and musical literature.

Perhaps it is to this flourishing state of the book and music trade that we owe the strange phenomenon that almost every person who has heard or read anything, feels he must promptly attempt poetry or composition himself. I have often heard the complaint from university professors that their students no longer attend to their studies, but play at writing or composing. This was particularly the case at Leipzig, where the book trade is so closely allied to erudition that one might almost ask which has our modern education most in hand, the university or the book trade. Plainly, one can learn as much or even more from books than from professors, since these latter are so short-sighted as to publish in cheaply priced monographs their whole stock-in-trade of information. The passion of our lecture-glutted students for

writing verse and tunes, upon the other hand, could be compared with that extraordinary love of play-acting which, from
the dawn of German histrionic art to the beginning of our present
century, has lured sons and daughters from the most respectable
families. Our young people appear to have grown somewhat
philistine as regards acting, perhaps from the fear of making
themselves ridiculous on the stage; a personal discomfiture now
more and more relinquished to the Jews, who seem to take less
account of unpleasant experiences. But poetry and composition
can be indulged in quite quietly and peaceably at home: nor
do we notice how foolish our lyrical outpourings make us look
in print, since luckily no reader discovers this either. The thing
does not become perceptibly absurd until it is read aloud. In my
time the Leipzig students used to torment a poor devil by persuading him to declaim his poems in return for his bills being
paid. They had his portrait lithographed, above the motto: 'Of
all my sufferings, Love is the cause'. Some years ago I told the
story to a well-known poet of our day, who has since taken a
strange dislike to me: I learnt too late that he had a new volume
of poems in the press at that very moment.

As for the German 'Poets' Corner', it appears that, despite
the need to keep their machinery in constant use, the publishers
are growing more and more averse to lyric poems, since the
lyrical composers continue to set nothing more recent than
Du bist wie eine Blume or *Wenn ich dein holdes Angesicht* to
music. How matters stand with epic poetry, is difficult to judge.
A great deal of it is thrown upon the market, and, moreover, is
set to music for our Subscription Concerts by composers who
hope one day to have an opera produced: a course, alas, found
hitherto impossible with *Der Trompeter von Säckingen*![1] That
all this brings in much money is highly unlikely, for there are
still a great many Germans who never subscribe to such concerts.
Dramatic poems, on the other hand, do have a larger public, at
any rate when they are produced on the stage. But among
theatrical directors one meets the wildest craving for financial

[1] By Victor Nessler (1841-90).

returns; the barbaric justice of 'God's verdict' still prevails, and that is not so lightly bought. It is only in England that publishers have found it possible to make use of the theatre for ingenious advertising. The sole article of any service to the English music trade is a ballad modelled more or less on the street-singer's genre, which, if it is successful, is sold in several hundred thousands of copies to all the colonies as 'the very latest'. To launch this ballad, the publisher spends money on the composition of an entire opera, pays the manager for its performance, and then proceeds to give the inserted ballad out to all the barrel-organs of the land, till finally it is heard in every home where there is a piano. If one calls to mind our own *Einst spielt ich mit Zepter*,[2] one might think that German publishers were also no fools, and knew what they were about, with the complete *Zar und Zimmermann* : the 'Czar' finds work for the engravers, and he who 'plays the sceptre' pays them.

Nevertheless, the writing of complete dramas appears to exercise an immense charm for young and old alike, and it is remarkable how every author believes he has done wonders with the stalest subject, under the illusion, no doubt, that it had never been properly treated by his predecessors. The five-foot iambic, jogging on in time-honoured fashion, is still used to confer upon the diction its true poetic flavour. Naked prose, however, the less distinguished the better, affords more chance of the piece being accepted by directors. The five-footed dramatist has therefore to depend, in general, on the favour of the publisher, who is forced to keep on printing; so that one may assume his only interest is in art as a hobby. I scarcely think that this is how really great poets are born. How Goethe and Schiller began, God only knows, unless some information could be gleaned from the firm of Cotta, who once declined to issue my *Collected Works* because they still had their hands so full with Goethe and Schiller.

But are not all these things mere poetic foibles? Though a true inhabitant of our Poets' Corner may in youth produce verses and rhymes in childlike imitation of the birds in the trees, when

[2] In Lortzing's *Zar und Zimmermann*.

he assumes the *toga virilis* he blossoms into a novelist, and at
last learns his business. Now the publisher seeks him out, and
so he begins to put his price up. He is in no hurry to hand his
three, his six or his nine volumes to the lending libraries: first
comes the magazine reader's turn. Even a political review
cannot decently subsist without a solid arts column with theatre
criticism and exciting fiction; and, on the other hand, what
receipts these newspapers drag in, and what a figure they can
pay! Engrossed in true creation, my friend Gottfried Keller
forgot in his day to bother about these newspaper-publishing
niceties; an already famous novelist, who regarded Keller as his
equal, most obligingly instructed him how to make a novel bring
in money. Manifestly the officious friend saw in the unbusinesslike
poet a terrible case of wasted energy, on which he could not look
without a pang. The incorrigible poet (his friends used to call him
'Auerbach's Keller')[3] did not in any case get very far in the
race for sales. It was only the other day that a second edition
of his novel *Der grüne Heinrich* appeared; it was first published
thirty years ago. Our wide-awake authors would consider this
a manifest failure, in fact, positive proof that Keller had not
risen to the occasion. They, of course, know better. And so our
Poets' Corner is so crowded that one cannot see the corner for
the books.

In this highly prosperous activity of our modern poets however, we find that element to which all poetry owes its being, its
very name. The narrator is the real poet, whereas the subsequent
formal elaborator of the narrative should rather be regarded as
the finishing artist. Only, if we are to accord to our flourishing
novelists the significant status of genuine poets, that significance
itself must first be somewhat more precisely defined.

The old world, strictly speaking, knew but one poet, and
named him Homeros. The Greek word 'poietes', which the
Latins were unable to translate and therefore reproduced as
'poeta', recurs naïvely among the Provençals as 'trouvere', and

---

[3] Auerbach's Beer Cellar in Leipzig, where a scene in Goethe's *Faust* takes
place.

suggested to our medieval Germans the term of 'finder'. Gottfried
von Strassburg called the poet of *Parsifal* a 'Finder wilder Märe'
('finder of strange tales'). That 'poietes', whom Plato claimed
to have been the true god of the Greeks, would seem to have
been preceded by the 'seer', much as the ecstatic showed Dante
the way through hell and heaven in his vision. But the unique-
ness of the Greeks' great poet seems to have been that he was
both seer and poet; for this reason they also represented him
as blind, like Tiresias. Those who were meant by the gods to
see not the appearance, but the very essence of the world, were
given sealed eyes. Thus they could reveal to the sight of mortals
that truth which, seated in Plato's figurative cavern with their
backs turned to the world, they could hitherto only see in
shadows. This poet, as seer, saw, not reality but the truth behind
reality; and because he could relate it so faithfully to his listeners,
it seemed to them just as clear and tangible as something which
they had held in their own hands. This made the seer a poet.

Was he an 'artist' as well?

He who seeks to demonstrate the art of Homer, will have as
hard a task before him as if he undertook to show the genesis of
a human being by referring to the laborious experiments of
some professor of Chemistry or Physics. Nevertheless, the work of
Homer is not simply a reproduction of Nature, but something
infinitely higher, perhaps the plainest manifestation of a godlike
knowledge of all that lives. Yet Homer was not an artist. The
poets who came after him were artists, and that is why he is
called the 'Father of Poetry'. All Greek genius is nothing other
than an artistic imitation of Homer, for the purpose of which that
technique was first discovered and matured which we now call
an 'art', thoughtlessly including in this 'art of poetry' as we do
both the 'poietes' and the 'Finder der Märe'.

The *ars poetica* of the Latins may indeed rank as art, and
from it the whole artifice of verse- and rhyme-making which we
know today may well be derived. Dante was gifted with the
seer's eye, for he saw the divine, though not the clear godlike
forms; but when we come to Ariosto, things have dwindled to

the fanciful refractions of mere appearance. Cervantes, on the other hand, perceives behind the glimmerings of such arbitrary fancies the old poetic soul of the antique world, and sets that contrast palpably before us in the lifelike actions of two figures seen in dream. Then, as if recapturing Time itself, a Scotsman's 'second sight' develops into full clairvoyance of a world of history now lying lost to us in forgotten documents, and he, Walter Scott, tells us its facts as truthful fairy-tales recounted skilfully to listening children. But from that *ars poetica*, to which these geniuses owed nothing, has issued all that, since Homer, we have known as epic poetry. After Homer we have to seek the genuine epic fount in folk tales and sagas, where we find it still entirely unspoilt by art.

There is no doubt that what emerges nowadays from magazines to line the walls of circulating libraries, does not have anything to do with either art or poetry. That which has been actually experienced has never at any time been able to serve as material for epic narration; and a gift for the purely imagined does not bestow itself on every writer of romances. A critic once blamed the departed Gutzkow for depicting a poet's love-affairs with baronesses and countesses, 'things of which he certainly could never have had any personal experience'; the author most indignantly replied by thinly-veiled allusions to similar episodes that had actually happened to himself. On neither side could the unseemly folly of our fiction writing have been more clearly exposed. Goethe, on the other hand, wrote his *Wilhelm Meister* as an artist to whom the poet had refused his collaboration in discovering a satisfactory ending; in his *Elective Affinities* the lyric elegist transformed himself into a seer of souls, but not as yet of living shapes. But what the imagination of Cervantes had conceived as Don Quixote and Sancho Panza, was transformed by Goethe's piercing talent into Faust and Mephistopheles; and these shapes beheld by him haunted this seeking artist like the unsolved key to an ineffable dream, which he hoped, inartistically but thoroughly sincerely, to solve in an impossible drama.

There may be something to learn from this, even for our German poets who feel neglected by their none too ardent publishers. For, alas, one must say to their novels, their imagination's ripest fruits, that they have sprung from neither life nor tradition, but simply from theft and translation. If neither the Greeks in their prime, nor the Italians or Spaniards, could extract from passing incidents the matter for an epic story, to modern writers this will presumably come still harder. The events witnessed by past generations were at least real phenomena; whereas we, in all that surrounds us and dwells in us, can find nothing but masquerades tricked out with rags of culture from the theatrical wardrobe, and tags from the historical museum. The gods have never granted the seer's eye which perceives that which lies beyond experience to any but their true followers, as we may see from Homer or Dante. But we have neither faith nor godliness.

So much for poetry. Now let us see what art can offer in these days of cultural progress.

We came to the conclusion that all Greek genius was merely an artistic reshaping of Homer, whilst in Homer himself we refused to recognise the artist. Yet Homer knew the bards; he himself was perhaps even one of them. The chorus of youths approached the mazes of the imitative dance to the sound of heroic songs. We know the choral chants of the priestly ceremonies, the dithyrambic choral dances of the Dionysian rites. What was originally the inspiration of the blind seer became the intoxicant for the wide-eyed ecstatic, before whose reeling gaze reality dissolved once more into godlike twilight. Was the musician an artist? I rather think he created all art, and became its first law-giver.

The shapes and deeds perceived by the piercing inner eye of the blind poet bard could be experienced by ordinary mortals only by means of some ecstatic transformation of their usual faculty of seeing nothing but the physical reality : the movements of the represented god or hero are, of necessity, governed by other laws than those of common daily need, by laws established on the rhythmic ordering of harmonious tones. The fashioning of tragedy really belonged no longer to the poet but to the lyrical composer. There was not one shape, one deed in the tragic myth, that had not been beheld before by the godlike poet, and passed on to his people. Now they were seen by the eyes of mortal men, but enhanced by the magic of music. The lyric tragedian was therefore not a poet, but through mastery and use of the highest art he recreated the world the poet had beheld, and transported the people themselves to a state of heightened perception. Thus music became the means of expression of godlike vision, for every aspect of that vision. It was the supreme ecstasy of the Hellenic spirit. What remained when it had sobered down was nothing but a state of fragmentation – no longer art, but the arts – among which the art of poetry was eventually to present the strangest aspect, retaining for the position, length or brevity of syllables the canons of the musical lyric, without any idea of how it had sounded. These Odes have come down to us. Along with other prosaic conceits of the *ars poetica*, they too are labelled as poetry, and down through the ages people have sweated to produce such verses, words and syllables, in the belief that if these look no more than somewhat glib in the eyes of others, and finally in their own eyes, they have really written poetry.

We need not linger with this *ars poetica*, for we shall not find poetry there. With its practice, wit invaded poetry : the old didactic sentence, which could still run along lines of sacred or profane melody, as in the oracles of Pythia, became an epigram. It was here that artistic verse, with its really clever modern rhymes, found fit employment. Goethe, who attempted everything, even, to his own disgust, the hexameter, was never happier in verse or rhyme than when these served his wit. Indeed one cannot say that the discarding of this artifice of witty verse has improved our poets. Had *Der Trompeter von Säckingen*, for instance, had an injection of wit, that epic might not have gone through sixty editions, but it would probably have made pleasanter reading. The jingling rhymes of Heine, on the other hand, still yield a certain pleasure. On the whole, our generation's love of verse-making appears to spring from an innate imbecility, to which the attention of parents and tutors should be directed. If after reading through our youthful poets you light upon a young Ovid who really can write verses, by all means allow him to do so, as we still prefer the witty epigrammatist in literature, though not in music.

Although the task is an extremely difficult one, the present writer has tried from time to time to throw some light on the subject of music, but not as yet upon composition itself.

Music is the most unwitty thing conceivable, and yet we now have almost nothing but witty composition. I suppose that this has come about out of affection for our dear *littérateurs*, Herr Paul Lindau in particular, who only asks for amusement from all art, so I am told, since otherwise it bores him. But strangely, it is precisely our 'amusing' music that is the greatest bore of all (just think of those pieces called 'divertissement' at any of our concerts), whereas, say what you will, any completely unwitty symphony by Beethoven is absorbing, and always ends far too soon. Perhaps at bottom there is something lacking in our newspaper-reporters' system of aesthetics. It is not to be expected that we shall win over these champions of musical amusement to a different view; nevertheless, we ourselves can devote a few words to the unwitty aspect of music.

Have not the results of many inquiries already plainly taught us that music has indeed nothing to do with the common seriousness of life; that its character, on the contrary, is a sublime and grief-assuaging radiance; that though it smiles on us, it never makes us laugh? Surely we may consider the A-major Symphony of Beethoven the brightest thing that any art has ever brought forth : but can we fully appreciate this work in any but a state of the loftiest transport? Here a Dionysian feast is celebrated such as the Greeks are unlikely ever to have celebrated : let us plunge into the rushing tumult, the frenzy of delight. We never leave the realm of lofty ecstasy, in this high heaven above that earth where wit rakes up its meagre fancies. For here we are taking part in no masquerade – the sole amusement of our dull world of progress. Here we do not meet privy councillors dressed up as Don Juan, whose unmasking causes endless fun. On the contrary, those truthful shapes appear here that showed themselves in the great ranks of heroes to blind Homer. Deaf Beethoven calls them up again to enrapture us.

But there sits the journalist, forever seeking amusement. He has eyes only for material things; he perceives nothing, nothing at all. To him the time grows weary whereas to us the time of respite from the mundane world was far too short, too fleeting. But he must have his amusement! So, make jokes, you bold musicians, disguise yourselves and put your masks on! Compose, compose, even though no ideas occur to you! Why should it be called composing – putting together – if one has to have invention as well? But the more tedious you are, the more contrast you must put into your choice of masks : that will provide all the more amusement. I know famous composers whom you can meet today at popular concerts in the garb of a street-minstrel, tomorrow in the Hallelujah-peruke of a Handel, the day after as Jewish purveyors of czardas, and later as solemn symphonists. You laugh : and well you may, you witty hearers! But those gentlemen take themselves so seriously, so solemnly, that it becomes necessary to single out one of them and give him a diploma as the Prince of Serious Music of our day, expressly to stop your laughter. Perhaps, however, that only adds to it? For this serious prince of music would long ago have struck you as most wearisome, had you sly ones not taken a peep behind the mask, and discovered that it hid no such mighty dignitary, but merely someone like yourselves. So now you can go on playing masks again, pretending that you worship him, while really it amuses you to see how seriously he appears to accept your adulation. Yet what lies at the very bottom of this entertaining game of masks should be openly stated. The suave, but somewhat

philistine Hummel was once asked what beautiful landscape he
had in mind when he composed a certain charming rondo. To
tell the simple truth, he might have answered, 'A beautiful fugal
theme of Bach's in C-sharp'; but he was even more candid, and
confessed that the eighty ducats of his publisher had swum
before his eyes. A witty man; and one whom one might wish to
know!

Strictly speaking, however, the joke is not in the music, but
in the composer's pretence of having written well, with the
resulting quid pro quos. In the aforesaid masque one can scarcely
include Mendelssohn. He was not always frank of speech, in fact
he was fond of evasion, but he never lied. When asked what he
thought of Berlioz's music, he answered: 'Every man composes
as well as he can.' If he did not compose his choruses to
Antigone as splendidly as his *Hebrides Overture*, which I consider
one of the most beautiful musical works that we possess, the
reason was that it was the one thing he could not do. Because
of this, and, alas, of many similar instances, his followers may
have inherited from Mendelssohn the cold-blooded recklessness
with which they have tackled every kind of composition, like
that old General of Frederick the Great's who sang whatever
was set before him to the tune of the 'Dessauer March'. Thus
they merely reduce greatness with calm indifference to the
diminutive size of their own talent. It was certainly always their
intention to turn out something good. Unfortunately, their fate
has been the opposite to that of Mephistopheles, who always
willed the bad but did the good. Assuredly they each desired
to produce for once a real, true melody, one of those Beethoven-
ian shapes that seem to stand complete before us like a living
organism. But what was the use of *ars musicae severioris*, or even
of *musicae jocosae*, when the shape refused to be conjured up,
still less composed? All that they have produced looks so very
like Beethoven's music, that often it seems a straightforward
copy; yet the most artful concoction is unable even to produce an
effect remotely approaching the almost ridiculously insignificant
– which can be relied on at every concert to wake from lethargy

to sudden ecstasy a previously bored audience![4] Plainly maliciousness on the part of the public, which one must correct by strenuous application of the rod. My former colleague, the Dresden conductor, Gottlieb Reissiger, who was also the composer of 'Weber's Last Thought',[5] once bitterly complained to me that the very same melody which in Bellini's *Romeo e Giulia* always sent the public mad, in his own *Adèle de Foix* made no effect whatever. I fear that the composer of the 'last idea' of Robert Schumann would have a similar misfortune to bewail.

It seems we have a curious state of affairs here. I am afraid that to fathom it fully would lead us to the edge of mystical abysses, and make those who chose to follow us seem foolish in the eyes of our enlightened music world, just as, according to Carlyle's experience, the English regard all mystics as foolish. Luckily, however, the sorrows of our present musical world are largely explicable in the sober light of sociology, which pierces with its clarifying rays even the cosy covert of our groves of poets and bunches of composers. Everything is originally without guile, as once in Paradise. Mendelssohn's fine saying, 'Every man composes as well as he can', is a wise provision, and cannot really be bettered. Guile first begins when one wants to compose better than one can. As this cannot be, one gives oneself instead the air of having done so : one assumes a mask. Nor does that do so very much harm : things deteriorate only when a number of good people, principals and the like, are actually deluded by the mask, and the outcome is Hamburg banquets, Breslau diplomas and

---

[4] The opening of Beethoven's Fifth Symphony.
[5] One of Reissiger's piano pieces was misleadingly titled *Webers Letzter Gedanke*.

so forth. This illusion is only brought about by making people believe that one composes better than others who really do compose well. Yet even this is not so very dreadful, after all, for we may generalise Mendelssohn's dictum into 'Every man *does* what and how he can'. Why make such a fuss about the falsification of artistic judgment or musical taste? Is it not a mere bagatelle, compared with all the other things we falsify, wares, sciences, victuals, public opinions, trends in culture, religious dogmas, and so on? Are we to grow virtuous all of a sudden as regards music? When, a few years back, I was rehearsing the Vienna company in two of my operas, the first tenor complained to a friend of mine about the unnaturalness of my request that he should be virtuous for six whole weeks, and regular in his habits, since he knew quite well that as soon as I had gone away he could only keep going by the common operatic vice of loose living. This artist was right in denouncing virtue as an absurd demand. If our composers' delight in the show of their excellence, their chastity, and kinship to Mozart and Beethoven, were only possible without the need to vent their spite on others, one would grudge them nothing. Even this does not much matter in the long run, since the personal injury thus inflicted will heal in time. That the ready acceptance of the empty for the sound is cheapening everything we possess in the way of schools, tuition, academies and so on, by ruining the most natural feelings and misguiding the faculties of the rising generation, we may take as our punishment for the sloth and lethargy we wallow in. But that we should pay for all this, and have nothing left when we come to our senses, especially since we Germans pride ourselves on being a special race, this, to be frank, is abominable!

Enough has now been said for today about this last point, about the ethics of writing and composing.

Judaism in Music

Of the essays in this volume, *Judaism in Music* is the only one to have been published in English in recent years. But since, on that occasion,[1] it appeared in truncated form with several of its more scurrilous passages suppressed, I have thought it useful to reproduce it here in full. It is the product of a mind so contorted with hate and envy that it merits little consideration except as a reflection of Wagner's thought. But Wagner's admirers continually attempt to play down the composer's anti-Semitism, a trait which his detractors, of course, gleefully emphasise; and both sides tend to make use of carefully edited quotations from *Judaism in Music* for their own purposes. For this reason, also, it has seemed to me important that an unexpurgated text of this piece of obscene unreason should be made available again in English.

Das Judentum in der Musik was first published in 1850 in the *Neue Zeitschrift für Musik*, whose editor with careful disingenuity added the following footnote:

However foully her outward conformation, we have always considered it a pre-eminence of Germany's, a result of her great learning, that at least in the scientific sphere she possesses intellectual freedom. This freedom we now lay claim to and rely on, in printing the above essay, desirous that our readers may accept it in this sense. Whether one shares the views expressed therein, or not, the author's breadth of grasp will be disputed by no one.

The essay also appeared in Volume 5 of the collected works.

[1] *Wagner on Music and Drama,* ed. Goldman and Sprinchorn (London: Gollancz, 1970).

*

There was a reference in the *Neue Zeitschrift für Musik* recently to an 'artistic taste of the Hebrews', a phrase which of course was immediately attacked and defended. I consider it important to bring some clarity to the subject at the root of this discussion, a subject which critics either shy away from or become over-excited about. I shall not attempt to say anything new but shall explain people's instinctive dislike of Jewishness. What I refer to is simply what exists: I have no interest in imaginative theorising. Criticism destroys itself if, whether on the attack or the defensive, it attempts to do more.

As it is the popular dislike of Jewishness in the arts, particularly music, that I wish to explain, I shall make no reference to similar attitudes in religion and politics. In religion the Jews have long ago ceased to be our hated enemies, thanks to those Christians who have drawn people's hatred towards themselves. In politics proper we have never actually fought the Jews; in fact we have allowed Jerusalem to reign supreme, and have found to our dismay that Herr von Rothschild, too cunning to proclaim himself King of the Jews, has preferred to remain 'the Jew of Kings'. Society is another matter: as we move further towards social freedom we have felt the segregation of the Jews to be an injustice. But in proposing their emancipation, we were supporting an abstract principle rather than a concrete example. All our liberalism was a somewhat confused intellectual game, in so far as we proposed freedom for the Jews with no knowledge of the race, indeed with a distaste for any contact with them. Consequently our desire to give the Jews their rights sprang much more from principle than from real sympathy, and all the talking and writing about Jewish emancipation failed to mask our unwillingness to have any actual dealings with them.

So here we reach the starting-point of our enquiry: we shall attempt to understand the involuntary repulsion aroused in us by the personality and customs of the Jews, in order to justify this instinctive feeling which is obviously stronger and more overpowering than our desire to be free of it. We are deliberately distorting our own nature if we feel ashamed to proclaim the natural revulsion aroused in us by Jewishness. It is only quite recently that we appear to have realised how much more sensible it is to free ourselves from that self-deception and face the need to understand why, despite our pretended liberalism, we still feel this aversion. We discover to our astonishment that, while we have been fighting our irrelevant liberal battles up in the sky of illusion, the beautiful earth of reality has been taken over by someone no doubt very amused by our flights of fancy, someone who has too low an opinion of us to relax his hold on our material world. Completely unnoticed, the 'Creditor of Kings' has become the 'King of Creeds',[2] and we can only consider this King's plea for emancipation a peculiarly naïve one, since in reality it is we who require to fight for emancipation from the Jews. As the world is constituted today, the Jew is more than emancipated, he is the ruler. And he will continue to rule as long as money remains the power to which all our activities are subjugated. That the historical misery of the Jews and the criminal brutality of Christian German leaders have resulted in this power being in the hands of the sons of Israel requires no proof from me. But that the impossibility of our arts evolving further without complete re-organisation has given the artistic taste of our time into the custody of busy Jewish hands is the subject we must examine here more closely. What the vassals of the Roman world and the Middle Ages had sweated to pay to their overlords is today made use of by the Jew. Who bothers to notice that those innocent pieces of paper money are stained with the blood of countless generations? What the great artists have toiled to bring into being for two thousand unhappy years, the Jew today turns into an art business. Who perceives that the delicate

---

[2] A pun which is largely lost in English, depending on the two meanings of *Gläubiger*: 'believer' and 'creditor'.

little works of art are held together by the holy sweat from the brows of the geniuses of two thousand years?

We have no need to prove that modern art has been taken over by the Jews; this is a fact that leaps to the eye unbidden. And we should have to cover too great a field were we to undertake an explanation with reference to the history of our art. But if emancipation from Judaism seems to us a prime necessity, we must test our strength for this war of liberation. We shall not gain this strength merely by an abstract definition of the situation, but by an intimate knowledge of the nature of our deep-seated, involuntary feeling of repugnance for Jewish nature. By this unconquerable feeling, what we hate in the Jewish character must be revealed to us, and when we know it we can take measures against it. By revealing him clearly, we may hope to wipe the demon from the field, where he has been able to thrive only under the protective cover of darkness, a darkness that we good-natured Humanists ourselves have offered him to make his appearance less disgusting.

In ordinary life the Jew, who as we know possesses a God of his own, strikes us first by his outward appearance which, whatever European nationality we belong to, has something unpleasantly foreign to that nationality. We instinctively feel we have nothing in common with a man who looks like that. This must, in past times, have been upsetting to the Jew : nowadays, however, not only does he not mind this, his successes lead him to consider his difference from us as an advantage. Ignoring the moral aspect of this unpleasant freak of nature, and considering only the aesthetic, we will merely point out that to us this exterior could never be acceptable as a subject for a painting : if a portrait painter has to portray a Jew, he usually takes his model from his imagination, and wisely transforms or else completely omits everything that in real life characterises the Jew's appearance. One never sees a Jew on the stage : the exceptions are so rare that they serve to confirm this rule. We can conceive of no character, historical or modern, hero or lover, being played by a Jew, without instinctively feeling the absurdity of such an idea. (Our recent experiences of the work of Jewish actors can only be briefly discussed here. Since this essay was written, the Jews have succeeded in taking over not only the theatre but also the playwright's characters. A famous Jewish 'character actor' has done away with the poetic figures in Shakespeare, Schiller, and so on, and has substituted creatures of his own effect-laden and tendentious imagination. One's impression is as though the Saviour had been cut out of a painting of the Crucifixion, and replaced by a Jewish demagogue. This falsifying of our theatrical art is now complete, and this is why nowadays Shakespeare and Company are spoken of only in terms of their limited suitability for the stage.)[3] This is very important: a race whose general appearance we cannot consider suitable for aesthetic purposes is by the same token incapable of any artistic presentation of its nature.

Considerably more important is the effect upon us of Jewish speech, and this is the point at which we should consider Jewish influence on music. The Jew speaks the language of the country in which he has lived from generation to generation, but he always speaks it as a foreigner. As it is not our concern here to inquire into the reasons for this, we need blame neither Christian civilisation for having kept the Jews at bay nor the Jews for the consequences of their isolation. All we need do here is to throw some light on the aesthetic character of the resultant situation. To begin with, the fact that the Jew speaks modern European languages only as learnt and not as a native, makes it impossible for him ever to speak colloquially, authoritatively or from the depths of his being. A language, its expression and its evolution are not separate elements but part of an historical community, and only he who has unconsciously matured in this community can take any part in what it creates. But the Jew has stood quite apart from this community, alone with his Jehovah in a dispersed and barren stock, incapable of real evolution, just as

[3] This long parenthesis was added in 1869, nineteen years after the essay was written. Wagner was embittered by his benefactor Ludwig II's homosexual relationship with the young Viennese Jewish actor, Josef Kainz.

his own Hebraic language has been handed down as something dead. To create poetry in a foreign language has always been impossible, even for the greatest geniuses. Yet our entire European civilisation and art have remained foreign to the Jew; for he has taken no part in the evolution of either. At best he has been a cold, even a hostile onlooker. In this language, this art, the Jew can only imitate, he can create neither poem nor work of art.

We are repelled in particular by the purely aural aspect of Jewish speech. Contact with our culture has not, even after two thousand years, weaned the Jew away from the peculiarities of Semitic pronunciation. The shrill, sibilant buzzing of his voice falls strangely and unpleasantly on our ears. His misuse of words whose exact shade of meaning escapes him, and his mistakenly placed phrases combine to turn his utterance into an unbearably muddled nonsense. Consequently, when we listen to Jewish speech we are involuntarily struck by its offensive manner and so diverted from understanding of its matter. This is of exceptional importance in explaining the effect of modern Jewish music on us. When we listen to a Jew talking we are unconsciously upset by the complete lack of purely human expression in his speech. The cold indifference of its peculiar 'blabber' can never rise to the excitement of real passion. And if we, in conversation with a Jew, should find our own words becoming heated, he will always be evasive, because he is incapable of really deep feeling. He will never be excited by a mutual exchange of feelings with us, but only by matters of particular egotistic interest to his vanity or to his sense of profit. This, together with his manner of speaking, makes him to our ears more ridiculous than sympathetic. Although we may well think it possible that among themselves the Jews are able to express their feelings, particularly in domestic circles where purely human emotions come to the surface, this cannot form part of our present discussion since we are considering how the Jew, in life and in art, speaks to us.

If these defects in his manner of speaking render the Jew

almost incapable of artistic enunciation of his feelings, how much less capable he will be of expressing those feelings in song. Song is, after all, speech heightened by passion : music is the language of passion. If the Jew's already ridiculously vehement manner of speech is to be heightened, we shall be further alienated from him. If we were repelled by his appearance and his speech, his song will engage our attention only to the extent that we exclaim at so absurd a phenomenon. It is understandably in song, as the most indisputably vivid expression of personal feeling, that the offensive peculiarity of the Jewish nature reaches its peak. But it is for every aspect of art, not only those connected with song, that on a natural hypothesis we must consider the Jew unsuited.

The Jews' ideas on visual observation have rendered it impossible for any visual artist to emerge from them : their eyes have always busied themselves far more with practical affairs than with beauty or the spiritual substance of the material world. As far as I can discover, no Jewish architect or sculptor has appeared in our time. Whether recent painters of Jewish descent can really be considered creative artists, I must leave to the judgment of connoisseurs; presumably, however, the attitude of these artists to their art does not essentially differ from that of modern Jewish composers towards music, a subject we shall now consider in detail.

The Jew, completely incapable of communicating artistically with us either by his appearance or his speech, and least of all by his singing, has nevertheless succeeded in completely taking over public taste in that most popular of modern arts, music. To explain this situation, let us now consider how it was possible for the Jew to become a musician.

When our social evolution reached that turning-point at which the power of money to bestow rank began to be openly admitted, it was no longer possible to keep the Jews at bay. They had money enough to be admitted to society : after all, the craft of making money without working for it, in other words usury, was the only trade that had been bequeathed to them. Our modern culture, accessible to anyone with wealth, was, as a

luxury article, no longer denied to them. From now on, the
cultured Jew was met with in our society, and we must observe
how he differs from the ordinary, uncultured Jew. The cultured
Jew has gone to great trouble to rid himself of the obvious
distinguishing features of his fellow-believers : in many cases he
has even had himself baptised as a Christian. But this zeal has
not brought the cultured Jew the rewards he has hoped for. It has
served merely to isolate him and to render him the most heartless
of all men, thus losing him the sympathy we once felt for the
tragic history of his race. Having arrogantly dissociated himself from his former co-religionists, he has found it impossible
to attach himself to the society to which he has ascended. His
relationship is only with those who need his money, and money
has never yet proved a particularly thriving bond between men.
The cultured Jew stands alien and alienated in the midst of
a society he does not understand, with whose tastes and aspirations he is not in sympathy, and to whose history and evolution
he is indifferent. It is in this situation that we have seen the
emergence of Jewish thinkers. The thinker is the poet who looks
to the past; the true poet is the prophet who foretells. Only the
deepest and most heartfelt sympathy with a great, similarly
minded community, to whose unconscious feeling the poet gives
voice, can produce such a prophet. Completely cut off from this
community by the nature of his situation, equally completely
torn from all connection with his own race, the more distinguished
Jew can only consider his acquired culture as a luxury which
he does not know how to put to practical use. Our modern arts
have become part of this culture, particularly the art of music
which is the easiest to learn. Music, more so than the other arts,
has been raised by the efforts of great geniuses to heights from
which either, in new association with the other arts, it can express
the sublime or, separated from them, can deal in the emptiest
trivialities. Naturally, the expression of the cultured Jew in his
situation could only be indifferent and trivial, since his entire
artistic impulse was to him an unnecessary luxury. As his mood,
or some extra-artistic interest, dictated, so would he utter this

or that. He never felt a compulsion to say anything real, definite and necessary, he merely wanted to speak for the sake of speaking. Consequently, his concern was for the 'how', instead of the 'what'. No art today affords more opportunity of making statements with nothing real to say than music, since the greatest geniuses have already said all that music, as a separate art, was capable of saying. Once this had been said, there remained nothing but gabble whose painful accuracy and deceptive similarity was like that of parrots who repeat human speech, and was just as lacking in feeling and real expression as these foolish birds. In the particular case of our Jewish music-makers, this mimicry also exhibits the particular peculiarity of Jewish speech habits, which we have closely characterised above.

Although the peculiarities of Jewish speech and singing are most emphasised in the ordinary Jew who has remained faithful to his race, and the cultured Jew has taken the greatest pains to rid himself of them, yet they cling to him with an impertinent obstinacy. Though this misfortune can be explained by physiology, the reason for it is also connected with the social position of the cultured Jew. Our luxury arts may float in nothing but the air of our arbitrary imagination, but they retain a certain connection with their natural soil, the real spirit of the people. The true poet, in whichever art he creates, always derives his inspiration only from the faithful, loving contemplation of that instinctive life he can alone find amongst his people. Where does the cultured Jew find these people? Certainly not in that society in which he plays his artistic role. If he has any connection with this society, it can only be with that part of it which is cut off from the main, healthy stem. But the connection is a completely loveless one, and this lovelessness must become increasingly obvious to him when, for the sake of nourishing his art, he descends to the basic stratum of this society. Not only will he find everything here stranger and more difficult to understand, but the instinctive ill-will of the people will strike him here in all its naked force since, unlike the upper classes, they are neither weakened nor broken by self-advantage or by any interest in common with him. Spurned by the people, and in any case completely powerless to interpret its spirit, the cultured Jew is thrown back to his own racial roots, where at least understanding will come more easily to him. Like it or not, this is the fountain from which he must drink, yet all he finds there is a 'how', and not a 'what'. The Jew has never had an art of his own, so his life has never had any artistic side. Even today it offers to the seeker no universally human experience, but merely a peculiar method of expression, that which we have characterised above. The only musical expression his own people can offer the Jewish composer is the ceremonial music of their worship of Jehovah: the synagogue is the only source from which the Jew can draw popular motifs for his art which are intelligible to himself. However sublime we may care to imagine this musical religious service in its pure form, we cannot fail to notice that it has not come down to us in its purity. For thousands of years, it has not continued to evolve naturally. Like everything connected with Judaism, it has retained a fixed form. A form which is not subject to continual renewal must finally disintegrate. An expression whose content has long since ceased to be animated by living feeling becomes senseless and distorted. Who has not been convinced that the musical divine service in a popular synagogue is a mere caricature? Who has not had feelings of repulsion, horror and amusement on hearing that nonsensical gurgling, yodelling and cackling which no attempt at caricature can render more absurd than it is? In recent times, the spirit of reform has attempted to restore this singing to its former purity, but what has been attempted by the higher, reflective Jewish intellect can never, by its nature, be other than a fruitless attempt from above. It can never take root sufficiently for the cultured Jew, whose artistic need seeks just such a fount of life among his people, to find his guidance there. He seeks the instinctive, not the reflective which is his own product; and the only instinctive available to him is that same distorted expression.

If this return to his people is as involuntary, as imposed upon the cultured Jew by nature and necessity, as it is with all artists, then these unconsciously derived impressions will make their way into his art. The rhythms and melismata of the synagogue chant dominate his musical imagination in exactly the same way that instinctive knowledge of the modes and rhythms of our folk songs and dances shaped the creation of our vocal and instrumental music. There is in the whole range of our music, whether popular or classical, nothing that the cultured Jew can seize on except what generally charms him as being intelligible. But all that he finds sufficiently intelligible to make artistic use of is that which to some degree approaches the peculiarity of Jewish music. But if the Jew, in listening to either our folk or art music, were really to experience its heart and fibre, he would discover not the slightest resemblance to his own musical nature. Its utter unfamiliarity would so upset him that he would never find the courage to approach our style of art again. His very position amongst us, however, does not seduce the Jew towards so intimate an intrusion into our ways. Either intentionally, if he understands his relationship to us, or instinctively, if he does not, he listens only superficially to our music and its life-giving inner organism. By this cursory listening he only discerns superficial similarities to the one thing he can understand, that which is peculiar to his own nature. So, to him the accidental externals of our musical and artistic life must seem to be their essence; and when, as artist, he reflects them back to us, his creations necessarily appear to us strange, cold, peculiar, listless, unnatural and distorted. Thus, works of Jewish music often produce in us the kind of effect we would derive from hearing a poem by Goethe translated into that Jewish jargon we know as Yiddish.

Just as this dialect throws words and phrases together with extraordinary inexpressiveness, so does the Jewish musician fling together the various forms and styles of all composers and eras. Side by side in utmost chaos we encounter in his music the idiosyncrasies of every form. Since he is solely concerned with language and not with what is to be communicated, his babbling can be made bearable only by issuing every moment a new call to attention. Inner excitement, true passion, finds its individual

B

language in the moment it bursts through to the understanding. The Jew, as we have already pointed out, has no true passion, certainly none that can draw him towards artistic creativity. But where there is no passion, there is no repose : truly noble repose is nothing other than passion soothed by resignation. Where the repose has not been produced by passion, we find only inertia : and the opposite of inertia is only that prickling unrest which is to be found in Jewish music from beginning to end, except where it is replaced by this soulless, unfeeling inertia. The results of Jewish attempts at artistic creation must necessarily possess the qualities of coldness, indifference, triviality and absurdity, and we can only classify the Jewish period in modern music as one of final unproductivity, and of stability ossified.

By what example will this be made clearer to us? What better instance than the case of a composer of Jewish birth on whom nature had bestowed gifts such as were possessed by few before him? We have discovered while examining our antipathy towards the Jew, the contradictions in his nature both in itself and as it related to us, and his inability to enter into any real relationship with us or even to desire to develop the riches he had found on our soil. All this reaches a state of highly tragic conflict in the life and work of the prematurely deceased Felix Mendelssohn-Bartholdy. He showed us that a Jew can possess the greatest talents, the finest and most varied culture, the highest and most delicate sense of honour, and that none of these qualities can help him even once to move us to the depths of our being as we expect to be moved by art, and as we are when one of our own great artists simply opens his mouth to speak to us. It can be left to technical critics, who have probably reached the same conclusions as we have, to confirm, by reference to Mendelssohn's music, the undoubted truth of our remarks. It will suffice to mention here, in support of our general feeling, that in hearing a piece by this composer we were able to feel involved only when our craving for entertainment was catered for with the presentation and intermingling of the finest, smoothest and most skilful figures, as in the changing colours and forms of the kaleidoscope.

But never were we moved where these figures were intended to express the strong, innermost feelings of the human heart. In this later case, Mendelssohn even lost his sense of form : when he sought drama, as in his oratorios, he was forced quite openly to snatch at every formal detail which characterised the individuality of whichever forerunner he had chosen to copy. It is significant that the composer his inexpressive modern language preferred to imitate was our old master, Bach. Bach's musical language was formed at a period of our history when the universal musical language was striving towards clearer and more individual expression : pure formalism and pedantry had still so strong a hold that it was only due to the mighty force of Bach's genius that real human feeling broke through. The language of Bach stands in the same relationship to that of Mozart, and finally Beethoven, as the Egyptian Sphinx does to Greek figure sculpture : as the human face of the Sphinx strives to escape from the animal body, so the noble human features of Bach strive to dissociate themselves from the powdered wig. It is indicative of the unbelievably thoughtless confusion of the musical taste of our time that we can listen to both Bach and Beethoven and tell ourselves that there is only a formal, individual difference between them, and by no means a real cultural and historical difference. The fundamental difference, however, is easy to understand. Beethoven's language can be spoken only by a whole, complete, warm human being, because it is the language of a musician so accomplished that necessity forced him to push beyond absolute music, whose territory he had conquered to its farthest borders, to reveal to us the way to the fertilisation of all the arts through music, as her only possible way of successful development. On the other hand, Bach's language can easily be imitated by any skilful musician, though perhaps not in Bach's sense, because in it formality is still uppermost, and purely human expression has not yet become so preponderant that its 'what' can or has to be uttered unconditionally : it is still occupied in developing the 'how'. The flimsiness and arbitrariness of our musical style have been emphasised, if not actually created, by Mendelssohn's tendency to enunciate as interestingly and spiritedly as possible an obscure and almost non-existent content. Beethoven, the last of our musical geniuses, strove with the deepest feeling and the most miraculous gifts to give clear and certain expression to the inexpressible by the sharply defined form of his music. Mendelssohn on the other hand, in his music reduces these achievements to fantastic, fleeting and shadowy forms, whose indefinite, shimmering colours excite our capricious powers of imagination but which hardly disturb our purely human inner feelings, and certainly cannot hope to fulfil them. Only where an oppressive feeling of this inadequacy seems to overpower the composer's mood and compel him to express a soft and melancholy resignation, is Mendelssohn able to reveal another characteristic trait : in the subjective sense of a delicate individuality that confesses to its own powerlessness. This, as we have said, is Mendelssohn's tragic conflict; if, in the realm of art, we are to extend our sympathy to pure personality, we must not deny a large measure of it to Mendelssohn, even though the force of that sympathy may be weakened by the reflection that in Mendelssohn's case tragedy hovered around him rather than coming to strike him into a state of real, sorrowful and purifying awareness.

No other Jewish musician, however, can awaken a like sympathy in us. A widely renowned Jewish composer of our time[4] has introduced his productions to a section of our public whose confused musical taste, though he may not have caused it, has certainly proved profitable to him. The audience of our modern operatic theatre has for some time now gradually been led away not only from real works of dramatic art but from all works of good taste. Our places of entertainment are now filled mainly by that section of our society which merely seeks diversion from boredom. The disease of boredom, however, cannot be cured by doses of art, for it will merely transform itself into another form of boredom. But that famous operatic composer has made the nurturing of that delusion his artistic

[4] Meyerbeer.

aim in life. There is no point in describing in detail the artistic means he has used to achieve this aim. It is sufficient to note that his success reveals he knew how to deceive. He did so by foisting on to his bored audience[5] that jargon we have already mentioned, and by persuading it to accept as a smart, modern utterance something which was utterly foolish and trivial. That this composer also contrived various shocks and effective emotional situations need surprise no one who understands how desperately a bored audience longs for this kind of thing. Nor is it astonishing that he succeeded in this aim : it is obvious that, under such conditions, he was bound to prosper. Indeed, this deceiving composer goes so far that he deceives himself, and perhaps just as deliberately as he deceives his bored listeners. We really believe that he would like to create and yet at the same time realises that he cannot. To avoid this painful conflict between intention and ability, he writes operas for Paris, and sends them on tour around the world : the most certain method, nowadays, of achieving artistic success without being an artist. Under the weight of this self-deception, which may not be so easy to bear as one might think, he appears to us in an almost tragic light. But his purely personal wounded feelings give an appearance of tragicomedy, just as the uninteresting and the absurd are the distinguishing Jewish characteristics which the famous composer reveals in his music.

From a more detailed consideration of the facts set out above, which we have learnt to interpret in the light of our insuperable aversion to Jewishness, we can arrive at a proof of the incompetence of our present-day composers.

Had the two Jewish composers mentioned[6] really helped our

[5] Whoever has observed the insolent absent-mindedness and indifference of a Jewish congregation during the musical part of divine service in the Synagogue can understand why a Jewish opera composer is not at all offended by the same kind of behaviour in the opera house, for it must there seem less inadmissible to him than in the house of God. (Wagner's note)

[6] The attitude adopted by other Jewish musicians and also by all the cultured Jews towards their two most famous composers is characteristic. To the followers of Mendelssohn, that famous opera composer (Meyerbeer)

music to develop, then we should have had to admit that our inability to keep pace with them was due to some unexpected organic deficiency. But this is not so : on the contrary, compared with previous artistic eras, our own has, if anything, increased its musical possibilities. The deficiency lies in the spirit of our art itself, which longs for a different form of expression from that which, with difficulty, prevails at present. The incapacity of the art of music itself is exposed for us in the activities of that specially gifted musician Mendelssohn. But the emptiness of our whole society, its completely inartistic nature and desires, are clearly implied by the successes of that famous Jewish opera composer. These are the important points which must finally be drawn to the attention of all those who are sincerely interested in art. This is what we must examine, question, and endeavour to understand. Whoever shrinks from this task or turns away from this examination, either because he does not feel impelled to it or because he seeks to avoid something that might upset his thoughtless and unfeeling routine, is now to be included in this category of Jewishness in music. The Jews could never have taken over this art until they had proved, as they have, the insufficiency of its inner life. As long as the separate art of music possessed a really organic need for life, up until the time of Mozart and Beethoven, there were no Jewish composers to be found : it was impossible for an element completely foreign to this living organism to take any part in its growth. Only when a body's inner death is evident can outside elements gain entry, and then only to destroy it. Then the flesh of that body is

is a horror : their sense of honour leads them to feel how greatly in the opinion of the more cultured musicians he has compromised Judaism, and so they are pitiless in their condemnation. The adherents of that composer are much more cautious about Mendelssohn, contemplating his good luck in our superior musical world with more envy than evident ill-will. A third category, that of the Jews who just go on composing, is desirous of avoiding all trace of scandal among themselves in order that their methods of composition should not be upset in any way. The undeniable successes of the great opera composer they take note of, admitting his works to be not entirely without merit, although by no means admirable or even 'solid'. Really, the Jews are far too clever not to know the ins and outs of their situation. (Wagner's note) transformed into a swarming colony of worms. But who, looking at it, could imagine such a body to be alive? The true life, in other words the spirit, has fled elsewhere. This is what life is about. Only in true life can we too find the spirit of art again : not within its worm-infested corpse.

I have said that the Jews have produced no real poet. We must now consider Heinrich Heine. In the period when Goethe and Schiller flourished we certainly knew of no Jewish poets. But when our poetry turned into a lie, when it seemed that almost anything but a true poet could emerge from our completely unpoetic way of life, then it became possible for a very gifted Jewish writer of poems to reveal, in a most fascinating manner, the endless acidity and Jesuitical hypocrisy of our versifying which still thought of itself as poetry. He even poured scorn on his famous musical Jewish contemporaries for their artistic pretensions. Nothing deceived him. By the remorseless demon of denial of all that seemed fit to be denied, he was driven on without respite, through all the illusion of our modern self-deception, to the point where he deluded himself into poetry. His reward was that his poetic lies were set to music by our composers. He was the conscience of Judaism, just as Judaism is the defaming conscience of our modern civilisation.

We must mention one other Jew who appeared among us as a writer. From his Jewish isolation he came to us seeking redemption. He did not find it, and discovered that he could attain it only when we too were redeemed and became real men. To become one of us, however, the Jew has first to renounce Judaism. Börne did this. Yet even he teaches us that this redemption cannot be achieved easily or in comfortable complacency, but only by sweat, want, anguish and the depths of sorrow and suffering. Without a backward glance, take part in this work of redemption through self-denial, for then we are one and indivisible. But remember that your redemption from the curse laid on you can be achieved by only one thing, and that is the redemption of Ahasuerus – decline and fall!

What is German?

Was ist Deutsch?, though written in 1865, was not published until 1878 when it appeared in the February issue of the *Bayreuther Blätter*. It is also to be found in Volume 10 of the collected works.

*

An attempt to gain a clear idea of what is really to be understood by the expression 'German' has often weighed upon my mind.

The patriot frequently introduces his nation's name with unqualified admiration; the mightier a nation is, however, the less store it seems to set on repeating its own name with this show of reverence. It happens far less often in the public life of England and France, that people speak of 'English' and 'French' virtues; whereas the Germans are always alluding to 'German depth', 'German earnestness', 'German fidelity' and the like. Unfortunately it has become apparent, in very many cases, that this attribution was not entirely justified; yet we should perhaps do wrong to suppose that the qualities themselves are mere figments of the imagination, even though their name be taken in vain. It will be best to look to history for the meaning of this idiosyncrasy of the Germans.

The word 'deutsch' (German), according to the latest and most exhaustive researches, is not the name of a specific people; there was not in the past a race that could claim the original title

'German'. On the contrary, Jacob Grimm[1] has proved that 'diutisk' or 'deutsch' means nothing more than that which is familiar to those of us speaking a mutually intelligible language. It was contrasted earlier with 'wälsch' (Welsh), the name used by the German tribes to denote properties associated with the Gaelic and Celtic tribes. The word 'deutsch' reappears in the verb 'deuten' (to point, indicate, or explain): thus 'deutsch' is what is clear (*deutlich*) to us, the familiar, the habitual, that which has been passed on from our fathers, or which has sprung from our soil. Now it is a striking fact that the peoples remaining on this side of the Rhine and the Alps began to call themselves by the name of 'German' only after the Goths, Vandals, Franks and Lombards had established their dominion in the rest of Europe. Whilst the Franks spread their name over the whole great conquered land of Gaul, and the races left on the near side of the Rhine consolidated themselves into Saxons, Bavarians, Swabians and Eastern Franks, it was only at the division of the empire of Charlemagne that the name 'Deutschland' made its first appearance : as the collective name for all the races who had stayed on this side of the Rhine. Consequently it denotes those people who, remaining in their ancestral seat, continued to speak their original mother tongue, whereas the races ruling in Romanic lands gave up that mother tongue. It is to the speech and the original homeland, then, that the idea of 'deutsch' is knit; and there came a time when the people of this name could reap the reward for their loyalty to their homeland and their speech, for it was the heart of that homeland that for centuries ceaselessly refreshed and revitalised the disintegrating foreign tribes. Moribund and weakened dynasties were strengthened with recruits from the primal stock at home. The East-Frankish Carlovingians succeeded the enfeebled Merovingians; from the degenerate Carlovingians,

---

[1] Jacob Grimm, the grammarian and author of *Deutsche Grammatik* (published 1819-37), set himself against the use of logical concepts in the analysis of a language and called observation the soul of grammar. He was, however, a careful collector rather than a great intuitive expositor. The famous *Kinder- und Hausmärchen*, by himself and his brother Wilhelm, were published in 1812-15.

in their turn, Saxons and Swabians took the sceptre of the German lands; and when the whole might of Romanised Frankdom passed into the power of the purely German stock, the strange but pregnant appellation 'the Roman Empire of the German Nation' arose. So, at last, the pride that bade us look into the past for consolation, amid the ruins of the present, was able to feed upon this glorious memory. No other great racial culture has fallen into the plight of building for itself a fanciful renown as wholeheartedly as have the Germans. What profit the obligation to build such a fantastic edifice from relics of the past might perhaps bring us, will only become clear if we first try to realise its drawbacks without prejudice.

There is no doubt that these drawbacks are found above all in the realm of politics. Curiously enough, the historic glory of the word 'German' attaches precisely to that period which was so fatal to the German essence, the period of the German's authority over non-German peoples. The King of the Germans had to fetch the confirmation of this authority from Rome; the Roman Emperor's crown did not strictly belong to the Germans. The journeys to Rome were hateful to them, and they could be induced to take part in them only as predatory marches, during which, however, their chief desire was a speedy return home. They sullenly followed the Roman Emperor into Italy, and most cheerfully their German princes back to their homeland. This situation explains the continual powerlessness of so-called German glory. The idea of this glory was an un-German one. What distinguishes the Germans proper from the Franks, Goths, Lombards and so on, is that the latter found pleasure in the foreign land, settled there, and commingled with its people to the point of forgetting their own speech and customs. The German proper, on the contrary, was always considered as a stranger by the foreign people, because he did not feel at home abroad; and strikingly enough, we see the Germans hated to this day in Italy and in Slavonic lands, as foreigners and oppressors, whereas the shameful truth cannot be denied that Germans quite willingly live under foreign domination, as long as they are not dealt with violently as far as their language and customs are concerned, as we have seen in the case of Alsace.

With the fall of external political might, i.e. since the disappearance of the Holy Roman Empire, which we mourn today as the foundering of German glory, there begins paradoxically the real development of the genuine German essence. Though it was connected with the development of all other European nations, the German homeland assimilated their influences, especially those of Italy, in so individual a manner that in the last century of the Middle Ages German fashions of dress actually became a pattern for the rest of Europe, whereas at the time of so-called German glory even the magnates of the German Reich were clad in Roman-Byzantine garb. In the German Netherlands, German art and industry were powerful rivals of Italy's most splendid development. After the complete collapse of the German psyche, after the almost total extinction of the German nation in consequence of the indescribable devastations of the Thirty Years' War, it was from within Germany itself that the German spirit was reborn. German poetry, German music, German philosophy, are nowadays esteemed and honoured by every nation in the world : but in his yearning after national glory the German, as a rule, can dream of nothing but a sort of resurrection of the Roman Empire, and the thought inspires the most amiable German with an unmistakable lust for mastery, a longing to gain the upper hand over other nations. He forgets how detrimental to the welfare of the German people that notion of the Roman State had already proved itself to be.

To gain a clear idea of the only policy by which the nation's welfare may be advanced, to be worthy of the name of German, we must first ascertain the true meaning and individuality of the essence of the Germanic spirit which we found to be the only prominent power in history itself. Therefore, continuing to think historically, let us consider more closely one of the weightiest epochs in the evolution of the German people – that crisis which Germany had to pass through at the time of the so-called Reformation.

The Christian religion belongs to no specific race: Christian dogma addresses human nature itself. Only in so far as it has grasped in its purity this content common to all men, can a nation today call itself Christian. However, a people can make nothing fully its own but what becomes possible for it to grasp with its inborn feeling, and to grasp in such a fashion that in the new it finds its own familiar self again. In the realm of aesthetics and philosophic criticism it may be clearly demonstrated, that it was predestined for the German spirit to assimilate the foreign, the primarily remote from it, in the utmost purity and objectivity of intuition. One may aver, without exaggeration, that the antique world, now universally known and understood, would have stayed unknown had the German spirit not recognised and expounded it. The Italians made as much of the antique their own as they could copy and remodel; the French, in turn, borrowed from this remodelling whatever appealed to their national feeling for elegance of form: the Germans were the first to apprehend its essentially human originality, to seize therein a meaning quite remote from usefulness, and therefore of use only for rendering the essentially human. Through its deep understanding of the antique, the German spirit developed a capacity for restoring the essentially human itself to its pristine freedom; not employing the antique form to display any given essence, but revealing new forms by an understanding of the antique conception of the world. To recognise this plainly, one should compare Goethe's *Iphigenia* with that of Euripides. One could say that the true idea of the antique has existed only since the middle of the eighteenth century, since Winckelmann and Lessing.

That the Germans would have apprehended the Christian dogma with equally pre-eminent clearness and purity, and would have raised it to be the only valid confession of faith, just as they had raised the antique to a dogma in aesthetics, is something that cannot be demonstrated. Perhaps, by evolutionary paths unknown to us, and unimaginable by us, the Germans might have arrived at this position; and certain attributes would seem to suggest that, of all others, the German spirit did, in fact, reach this point. In any case, we can see what hindered its solution of the problem, if we recognise what enabled it to solve a similar one in the region of aesthetics. For here there was nothing to hinder it : aesthetics were neither interfered with by the State, nor converted to its ends. With religion it was the reverse : it had become an interest of the State, and this State interest obtained its meaning and its guidance, not from the German, but quite definitely from the un-German, the Roman spirit. It was the incalculable misfortune of Germany that, about the time when the German spirit was ripening for its great task, the legitimate State interests of all German peoples were entrusted to the counsels of a prince to whom the German spirit was totally remote, to the most thorough-going representative of the un-German, Roman idea of the State : Charles V, King of Spain and Naples, hereditary Archduke of Austria, elected Roman Emperor and Sovereign of the German Reich, who was devoured by his ambition for world-supremacy, which he would actually have attained if he had been able to conquer France.[2] This sovereign had no other interest in Germany than to weld it together with his Empire, as a firmly ruled monarchy like Spain.

He first conceived the error that later doomed almost every German prince to misunderstanding of the German spirit; yet he was opposed by the majority of the princely rulers of that time, whose interest then coincided, as good fortune would have it, with those of the German folk-spirit. One cannot speculate about the way in which the actual religious question, too, might have been answered to the honour of the German spirit if Germany then had had a staunch patriotic ruler as emperor, such as the Luxemburgian Henry VII. As it happened, the original

[2] Charles V secured election as Holy Roman Emperor in 1519 at great expense and without consulting the *Cortes* of Spain. He waged several wars with France, whose ruler, Francis I, feared Habsburg domination of Europe.

Reformation movement in Germany did not result in separation from the Catholic Church; on the contrary, it was an attempt to strengthen and reknit the Church's general union, by putting an end to the hideous abuses of the Roman Curia, which were so wounding to German religious feeling. What good or world-shattering events might have emanated from this we can scarcely begin to imagine; but we have before us the results of the disastrous conflict of the German spirit with the un-German spirit of the German Reich's supreme controller. Since that time we have suffered a dire misfortune : a divided religion. None but a universal religion can be a really true religion. Divers confessions, politically established and ranged beside or against one another by contract with the State, simply bear witness to the fact that religion is in a state of dissolution. In that conflict the German race was brought close to total collapse : it almost reached breaking point through the outcome of the Thirty Years' War. If, therefore, the German princes had until then mostly worked in common with the German spirit, I have already shown how since that time, alas, our princes themselves almost completely lost their understanding of this spirit. The sequel is plain for us to see in the public life of our State today: the sterling German nature is withdrawing even farther from its origins. To a certain extent, the Germans are following their native phelgmatic bent, but at the same time they incline towards fantasticism : and since both the lordling and the lawyer are becoming quite out of date, the royal rights of Prussia and Austria have nowadays gradually to accustom themselves to being upheld by the Jews.

In this singular phenomenon, this invasion of the German nature by an utterly alien element, there is more than meets the eye. Here, however, we will only take note of that other nature in so far as its conjunction with us obliges us to become quite clear as to what we have to understand by the German nature which it exploits. It everywhere appears to be the duty of the

Jew to show the nations of modern Europe where there may be a profit they have overlooked, or not made use of. The Poles and Hungarians did not understand the value to themselves of a national development of trade and commerce : the Jew displayed it, by appropriating that neglected profit. None of the European nations had recognised the boundless advantages, for their nation's general economy, of an ordering of the relations of labour and capital in accordance with the modern spirit of bourgeois enterprise : the Jews seized their opportunity and the plundered and dwindling prosperity of those nations is now fed upon by the enormously wealthy Jewish banker.[3] How adorable, how beautiful is that foible of the Germans which forbade their making personal profit out of the inwardness and purity of their feelings and responsibilities, particularly in their public and political life : that profit here, as well, was neglected, could be apparent to none but a mind which misunderstood the very essence of the German nature. The German princes supplied the misunderstanding, the Jews exploited it. Since the new birth of German poetry and music, the princes only needed to follow the example of Frederick the Great, to make a fad of ignoring these arts, or wrongly and unjustly judging them by French yardsticks, and consequently allowing no influence to the spirit which they manifested – it only needed this to throw open to the spirit of alien speculation a field wherein it saw much profit to be reaped. It is as though the Jew had been astounded to find such a store of mind and genius yielding no returns but poverty and lack of success. He could not conceive, when the Frenchman worked for *gloire*, the Italian, for the *denaro*, why the German did it simply '*pour le roi de Prusse*'. The Jew set right this bungling of the Germans, by taking German intellectual labour into his own hands; and thus we see an odious travesty of the German spirit upheld today before the German people as their imputed likeness. It is to be feared that, before long, the nation may really take this simulacrum for its mirrored image : then

[3] See introductory note to *Judaism in Music*, regarding Wagner's anti-Semitism.

one of the finest natural dispositions in all the human race will
have been done to death, perchance for ever.

We have to inquire how to save Germany from such a shameful fate, therefore we shall first try to outline the characteristics
of the genuine German nature.

Once more, let us briefly but plainly recite the external historical facts of the German nature. 'Deutsch' is the title given to
those Germanic races which, upon their natal soil, retained their
speech and customs. Even from beautiful Italy the German yearns
for his homeland. Hence he forsakes the Roman Emperor, and
clings more closely and trustingly to his native Prince. In rugged
woods, throughout the lengthy winter, by the warm hearth fire
of his turret chamber soaring high into the clouds, for generations he keeps alive the deeds of his forefathers; the myths of
native gods he weaves into an endless web of sagas. He does
not ward off the influences infiltrating from abroad; he loves
to journey and to look. Full of the strange impressions, however,
he longs to reproduce them; he therefore turns his steps towards
home, for he knows that here alone will he be understood : here,
by his own hearth, he tells what he has seen and experienced in
the outside world. Roman, Gaelic, French books and legends he
transposes for himself, and whilst the Latins, Gaels and French
know nothing of him, he keenly studies all their ways. But his
is no mere idle gaping at the foreign, merely for the sake of it;
his intention is to understand it in a German fashion. He
translates the foreign poem into German, in order to gain an
inner knowledge of its content. In doing so he strips the foreign
of its accidentals, its externals, of all that to him is unintelligible,
and makes good the loss by adding just so much of his own
externals and accidentals as is necessary to set the foreign
object clearly before him. In these endeavours, he makes the
foreign work yield a picture of its purely human aspects. Thus
Parsifal and *Tristan* were shaped anew by Germans : and whilst
the originals have become mere curiosities, of no importance
save to the history of literature, in their German counterparts we
recognise poetic works of imperishable value.

In the same spirit, the German borrows for his home the civic virtues of other countries. Beneath the castle's shelter, expands the burghers' town; but the flourishing town does not work against the castle. On the contrary, the 'free town' renders homage to the Prince; the industrial burgher decks the castle of his ancient lord. The German is conservative: his treasure bears the stamp of past ages. He hoards the old, and knows how to use it. He is fonder of keeping than of winning: the new has value for him only when it serves to deck the old. He craves for nothing from without, but he will not allow hindrances from within.

He does not attack, neither will he brook attack. Religion he takes in earnest: the ethical corruption of the Roman Curia, with its demoralising influence on the clergy, cuts him to the quick. By religious liberty he means nothing other than the right to deal honestly and in earnest with matters of the spirit. Here he waxes warm, and argues with all the passion of the peaceful man roused to action. Politics are involved in this: shall Germany become a Spanish monarchy, the free Reich be trodden underfoot, German princes be turned into mere courtiers? No other race has taken arms against invasions of its inner freedom, its own true essence, in the way that the Germans have. There is no comparison for the doggedness with which the German chose his total ruin, rather than accommodate himself to claims quite foreign to his nature. This is important. The outcome of the Thirty Years' War destroyed the German nation; yet, that the German race could rise again, is due precisely to that outcome. The nation was annihilated, but the German spirit had prevailed. It is the essence of that spirit, which we call genius in the case of highly gifted individuals, not to set too great a store by material gain. Although other nations were forced at last to compromise, in order to ensure profit through accommodation, this did not happen with the Germans. At a time when Richelieu forced the French to accept the laws of political advantage, the German nation appeared to be in a state of total collapse; but that which could never be made to bend before the laws of advantage lived on and bore its people to fresh heights: the German spirit.

With the race reduced to a tenth of its former numbers, its significance could only survive in the memory of individuals. Even that memory had first to be revived and laboriously fed, to begin with, by the most prescient of minds. It is a wonderful trait of the German spirit that, whereas in its earlier period of evolution it had most intimately assimilated the influences coming from without, now, when it had quite lost the vantage-ground of outward political power, it recreated itself anew from its own inner strength. Recollection now became for it in truth a re-collection of the self, for it drew upon its deepest inner self for protection from the now immoderate outer influences. It was not a question of its external existence, for that had been ensured by the continuance of the German princes; indeed, did not the title of Roman-German Emperor still survive? But its truest essence, now ignored by most of these princes, was the German spirit's determination to preserve itself and quicken to new force.

In the French livery and uniform, with periwig and pigtail, and laughably decked out with imitations of French gallantry, the scanty remnant of the German people faced the future. The burgher, with his garnish of French flourishes, was about to abandon the German language to the peasant. Yet, when its native countenance, its very speech was lost, there remained to the German spirit one last, one undreamt-of sanctuary wherein its innermost heart could still be expressed. From the Italians the Germans had taken to themselves music. Whoever wishes to understand the wondrous individuality, the strength and meaning of the German spirit in one incomparably speaking image, should look searchingly at the otherwise puzzling, almost incomprehensible figure of that greatest of composers, Johann Sebastian Bach. He embodies in himself the history of the German spirit's inmost life throughout the gruesome century of the German people's almost complete extinction. Observe that head, ridiculously muffled in the French full-bottomed wig; behold that master, a wretched

organist and cantor, as he slinks from one Thuringian parish
to another, insignificant places scarcely known to us by name.
In his own lifetime he was so unheeded, that it required a whole
century to rescue his works from oblivion. He found music itself
pinioned in an art-form which was the very effigy of his age,
dry, stiff, pedantic, like a powdered wig set to notes. But see
what a real world the unfathomably great Sebastian built from
these elements! I merely draw attention to that creation; for it
is impossible to denote its wealth, its sublimity, its all-embracing
import, through any manner of comparison. If, however, we wish
to account for the amazing rebirth of the German spirit in the
field of poetic and philosophic literature also, we can do so only
by learning from Bach what the German spirit really is, where
it was to be found, and how it strove to shape itself anew, when
it seemed to have altogether vanished from the world. A bio-
graphy of Bach has recently appeared, and the *Allgemeine Zeitung* has reviewed it. I cannot resist quoting the following passages
from that review:

> With labour and rare willpower he struggles up from poverty
> and need to the topmost height of art, strews with full hands
> an almost incommensurable plenty of most glorious master-
> works, strews it on an age which can neither comprehend nor
> prize him, and dies beneath a burden of heavy cares, lonely
> and forgotten, leaving his family in poverty and deprivation.
> . . . The grave of the dispenser of music closes over the
> hard-working family man without a song or sound, because
> the penurious household cannot afford the grave-chant fee.
> . . . Might the reason, why composers so seldom find bio-
> graphers, lie partly in the circumstance that their end is
> usually so mournful, so harrowing?

And while this was happening with great Bach, sole harbourer
and new bearer of the German spirit, the courts of German
princes both large and small were swarming with Italian opera
composers and virtuosi, bought with untold wealth, who showered

on slighted Germany the leavings of an art that nowadays cannot
be accorded the slightest consideration.

Yet Bach's spirit, the German spirit, stepped forth from the
sanctuary of heavenly music, the place of its rebirth. When
Goethe's *Götz*[4] appeared, the joyous cry went up: 'That's
German!' And, beholding his likeness, the German also knew
how to show himself, and show the world, what Shakespeare –
whom his own people did not understand – is. This the German
spirit brought forth of itself, from its desire to grow conscious
of itself. And this consciousness told it what it was the first to
make known to the world: that the beautiful and noble does
not come into the world for the sake of profit, or even for the
sake of fame and recognition. Everything done in this spirit is
'deutsch'; that is why the German is great; and only what is
done in this spirit, can lead Germany to greatness.

Nothing can nurture the German spirit, or lead the German
race to greatness, but the understanding of its rulers. The German
race arrived at its rebirth, at an unfolding of its highest faculties,
through its conservative temper, its inward cleaving to itself, to
its own character. Once, it shed its life's blood for the preservation
of its princes. It is now for them to show the German race that
they are worthy of it; and in this realm where the German spirit
achieved its rebirth the princes must found their new alliance
with the people. It is high time the princes achieved this re-
baptism: because otherwise the whole of German public life is
threatened, as I have already pointed out. Woe to us and the
world, if this time the nation itself were saved, but the German
spirit vanished from the world!

How are we to imagine a state of things in which the German
race remains, but the German spirit has disappeared? This almost
inconceivable event is closer to us than we think. When I defined
the essence and functions of the German spirit, I had in mind a
happy development of the German people's most significant
attributes. But the birthplace of the German spirit is also the basis

[4] *Götz von Berlichingen*, which appeared in 1773, and was the first major
work of genius of the 'Sturm und Drang' movement.

of the German people's failings. The capacity to delve deep, and thence to observe lucidly and thoughtfully the outside world, always presupposes an urge towards meditation, which, in the less gifted individual, quite easily becomes a love of doing nothing, a positively phlegmatic condition. What in its happiest manifestation places us closest to the supremely gifted people of ancient India, may appear to give the masses the character of common Oriental sloth. Even the urge towards powerfulness can become a curse for us, by betraying us into a fantastic self-complacency. That Goethe and Schiller, Mozart and Beethoven have issued from the German nation, far too easily tempts the mass of middling talents to consider these great minds similar to themselves by right of birth, and persuades them into imagining themselves Goethes and Schillers, Mozarts and Beethovens. Nothing is more conducive to sloth and laziness than a high opinion of oneself, the idea that one is something intrinsically great and need take no pains to improve oneself. This tendency is very German, and hence Germans need to be awakened and compelled to help themselves, to act for themselves, more than any other race. But German princes and governments have done the very opposite. It was left to Börne the Jew[5] to sound the first challenge to the Germans' sloth; and albeit in this sense unintentionally, he thereby raised the Germans' great misunderstanding of themselves to a pitch of the most dire confusion. This was the misunderstanding that prompted the Austrian Chancellor, Prince Metternich, at the time of his leadership of German Cabinet policy, to assume that the aspirations of the German Burschenschaft were identical with those of the bygone Paris Club of Jacobins,[6] and to take hostile measures accordingly, which was most advantageous for the Jewish speculator who stood outside, seeking nothing but his own personal profit. This time, if he played his game well, that

[5] Ludwig Börne (1786-1837), the German journalist. He was an outspoken liberal and advocate of social and intellectual equality for the Jews. His *Briefe aus Paris* (letters from Paris, 1832-4) were filled with criticism of Prussia and were prohibited by the government.
[6] A prime force in the French Revolution.

speculator had only to infiltrate himself into the midst of the German people and State, to exploit it, and, in the end, not merely govern it, but make it completely his own.

After all that had gone before, it had now really become a difficult matter to rule in Germany. If the governments had made it a maxim to judge their peoples by the yardstick of French events, there soon arose also adventurers to teach the downtrodden Germans to apply French maxims to their estimate of the governments. The Demagogue had now indeed arrived : but what a doleful arrival! Each new Parisian revolution was promptly reproduced in Germany : understandably, since every new spectacular Paris opera had been immediately staged at the court theatres of Berlin and Vienna, which were a pattern for the whole of Germany. I have no hesitation in calling the subsequent revolutions in Germany entirely un-German. Democracy in Germany is purely a translated thing. It exists merely in the Press; and what this German Press is, one must find out for oneself. But, curiously enough, this translated Franco-Judaic-German democracy could really gain support from the misprised and maltreated spirit of the German people. To secure a following among the people, democracy put on a German face. 'Germanism', 'German spirit', 'German honesty', 'German freedom', 'German morals', became catchwords disgusting no one more than the truly cultured German, who had to stand in sorrow and watch the singular comedy of agitators from a non-German people pleading for him without allowing their client so much as a word in edgewise. The astounding lack of success of that so vociferous movement of 1848 is easily explained by the curious circumstance that the genuine German found himself, and his name, so suddenly represented by a race of men quite alien to him. Whilst Goethe and Schiller had spread the German spirit throughout the world, without so much as mentioning the German spirit, these democratic speculators fill every book- and print-shop, every so-called 'folk theatre', with vulgar, utterly vapid dummies, forever plastered with the accolade of 'deutsch', to deceive the easygoing crowd. And we have really gone so far, that we shall presently see the German people quite ruined by this. The national propensity to phlegmatic sloth is being lured into a fantastic satisfaction with itself, while playing this shameful comedy; and the thoughtful German soul cannot look without a shudder upon those foolish festive gatherings, with their theatrical processions, their silly speeches, and the pompously empty songs by which the German race is being made to imagine it is already something special, and that it does not need to make any endeavour in order to become so.

A Pilgrimage to Beethoven

The three stories, *Eine Pilgerfahrt zu Beethoven, Ein glücklicher Abend* and *Ein Ende in Paris,* first appeared in French translation in the *Revue et Gazette Musicale de Paris* in 1840 and 1841. The original German texts were subsequently published in the Dresden *Abend Zeitung* in 1841. They are also in Volume 1 of the collected works.

For these stories, the twenty-seven-year-old Wagner invented the character of an unknown, middle-aged German composer who worships Beethoven, and makes a pilgrimage from the north of Germany to Vienna to see the great man. In the second story, the unknown composer arrives in Paris where, after a year or two of vain attempts to make a career in music, he dies in extreme poverty, as related in the final story. The first story, *A Pilgrimage to Beethoven,* is written in the first person as by the hapless composer himself. When it was published in German, Wagner prefaced it with this note:

> Shortly after the modest funeral of my friend Robert who died recently in Paris, I began to write a brief history of his sufferings in that glittering metropolis, in accordance with the deceased's wishes. Among his papers I found this fond narration of his journey to Vienna to visit Beethoven, which confirmed much that I had already noted down. Thus I decided to print that fragment of his diary to preface my own account of his mournful end, since it deals with an earlier period of his life, and may also help arouse interest in my departed friend.

A Happy Evening was actually the last of the three stories to be published. I have, however, placed it second, so that the trilogy can end with the death of Robert in *An End in Paris.* In the second and third stories the narrator is ostensibly Wagner himself.

*

Want-and-care, thou patron-goddess of the German musician, unless he happens to have risen to the rank of Kapellmeister at a court theatre; Want-and-care, thine be the name first lauded in this as in every reminiscence from my life! Yes, let me sing of thee, thou staunch companion of my days! Faithful hast thou been to me, and never left me; the smiles of Inconstancy thou hast ever warded off, and shielded me from Fortune's scorching rays! In deepest shadow hast thou hidden from me the empty baubles of this earth : have thanks for thy unwearying attachment! Yet, if thou canst, I beg thee some day to see another favourite; for, if only out of curiosity, I fain would learn for once how life might be *without* thee. At least, I beg thee, plague especially our political dreamers, the madmen who are breathless to unite our Germany beneath *one* sceptre. Think of it : there would then be but one court theatre, one solitary Kapellmeister's post! What would become of my prospects then, my only hopes, which even now, when German royal theatres exist in plenty, hover but dimly and in shadow before me. But I perceive I am becoming blasphemous. Forgive, my patron-goddess, the dastardly wish just uttered! Thou knowest my heart, and how entirely I am thine, and shall remain thine, were there a thousand royal theatres in Germany. Amen!

Without this daily prayer of mine I begin nothing, least of all the story of my pilgrimage to Beethoven!

In case this weighty document should be published after my death, however, I further consider it necessary to say who I am; since much that it contains might otherwise not be understood. Read on then, world and executor!

I was born in a medium-sized town in the middle of Germany.

I am not quite certain what I was originally intended to be; I only remember that one night for the first time I heard a symphony of Beethoven's performed, that it set me in a fever, that I fell ill, and that on my recovery I had become a musician. This circumstance may perhaps account for the fact that, though in time I became acquainted with much beautiful music, I have loved, honoured and worshipped Beethoven before all others. Henceforth I knew no other pleasure than to plunge so deeply into his genius that at last I thought myself part of it; and, as such, I began to respect myself, to acquire more elevated thoughts and views, in short to develop into what sober people call an idiot. My madness, however, was of a very good-humoured sort and did no harm to anyone. The bread I ate, in this condition, was very dry, and the liquid I drank most watery, for giving music lessons yields only poor returns.

Thus I lived for some time in my garret, till it occurred to me one day that the man whose creations I revered above all else was still *alive*. I could not understand why I had never thought of this before. It had never struck me that Beethoven could exist, could be eating bread and breathing air just like the rest of us. Yet this Beethoven was actually living in Vienna, and he too was a poor German musician!

My peace of mind was gone. My every thought turned into one wish: *to see Beethoven*! No Mohammedan more devoutly longed to journey to the grave of his Prophet, than I to go to the house where Beethoven lived.

But how was I to set about achieving my object? The journey to Vienna was a long one, and money would be needed; I, poor devil, hardly earned enough to stave off hunger! So I must think of some unusual way of raising the necessary funds. I carried a few pianoforte sonatas, composed in the master's style, to a publisher; but the man made it plain in a few words that I and my sonatas were no good. He gave me the advice, however, that if I wanted some day to earn a few shillings with my compositions, I should begin by gaining a small reputation with galops and pot-pourris. I shuddered, but my yearning to see

Beethoven won the day. I did compose galops and pot-pourris, though in all that time I could never bring myself to cast one glance in Beethoven's direction for fear it should defile him.

Unfortunately, however, these earliest sacrifices of my innocence did not bring me any remuneration, for my publisher explained that first I must make something of a name for myself. I shuddered again, and fell into despair. That despair brought forth some capital galops. I actually received money for them, and at last believed I had amassed enough to execute my plan. But two years had elapsed, and all the time I was afraid that Beethoven might die before I had made my name with galops and pot-pourris. Thank God! he survived to see the glitter of my success! Immortal Beethoven, forgive me my renown; it was won in order that I might see you!

Oh joy! my goal was in sight. Was there a happier man than I? Now I could put a knapsack over my shoulder and set out for Beethoven at once. A holy awe possessed me when I passed through the gate and turned my footsteps southwards. I would gladly have taken a seat in the coach, not because I feared foot-soreness (what hardships would I not cheerfully have endured for such a goal!) but because I should thus have reached Beethoven sooner. My fame as galop-composer, however, did not enable me to pay my carriage fare. So I bore all discomfort, and thought myself lucky to have got so close to my goal. Oh, what fantasies, what dreams I had! No lover, returning to his youthful love after years of separation, could have been happier.

And so I came to beautiful Bohemia, the land of harpists and wayside singers. In a little town I found a troop of strolling musicians. They formed a tiny orchestra, composed of a 'cello, two violins, two horns, a clarinet and a flute; there was also a woman who played the harp, and two other women with lovely voices. They played dances and sang songs; people gave them money and they journeyed on. In a beautiful shady place beside the highway I found them again; they had camped on the grass, and were taking their meal. I introduced myself by saying that

I too was a travelling musician, and we soon became friends. As they played dance-music, I bashfully asked if they knew my galops. God bless them! They had never heard of my galops. How happy this made me!

I inquired whether they played any other music besides dances.

'To be sure,' they answered, 'but only for ourselves; not for gentlefolk.'

They unpacked their music, and I caught sight of Beethoven's great Septet. Astonished, I asked if they played that, too.

'Why not?' replied the eldest. 'Joseph has hurt his hand and can't play the second violin today, otherwise we'd be delighted to give it at once.'

Beside myself, I snatched up Joseph's violin, promised to do my best to replace him, and we began the Septet.

O rapture! Here on the slope of a Bohemian highway, in the open air, Beethoven's Septet was played by dance-musicians with a purity, a precision, and a depth of feeling too seldom found among the greatest virtuosi! Great Beethoven, we brought thee a worthy offering.

We had just reached the Finale when, the road sloping up at this spot toward the hills, an elegant travelling-carriage approached slowly and noiselessly, and finally stopped close by us. An astonishingly tall, astonishingly blond young man lay stretched full-length in the carriage. He listened to our music with some attention, drew out a pocket-book and made a few notes. Then he dropped a gold coin from the carriage and drove away with a few words of English to his lackey; whence it dawned on me that he must be an Englishman.

This incident quite put us out; luckily we had finished our performance of the Septet. I embraced my friends, and wanted to accompany them; but they told me that they must leave the high road here and strike across the fields, to return to their native village for a while. Had it not been Beethoven himself who was awaiting me, I certainly would have kept them company. As it was, we bade each other a tender goodbye, and parted. Later it occurred to me that no one had picked up the Englishman's gold coin.

Upon entering the nearest inn for some sustenance, I found the Englishman seated before an ample meal. He eyed me up and down, and at last addressed me in passable German.

'Where are your colleagues?' he asked.

'They have gone home,' I replied.

'Take out your violin and play me something else,' he continued. 'Here's some money.'

That annoyed me. I told him I neither played for money, nor had I any violin, and briefly explained how I had fallen in with those musicians.

'They were good musicians,' put in the Englishman, 'and Beethoven's music was very good, too.'

Struck by this remark, I asked him if he played an instrument.

'Yes,' he answered, 'twice a week I play the flute, on Thursdays the French horn, and on Sundays I compose.'

That was a good deal, enough to astound me. In all my life I had never heard of travelling English musicians; I concluded that they must do very well, if they could afford to make their tours in such splendid style. I asked if he was a musician by profession.

For a long time he made no reply. Finally he drawled out that he had plenty of money.

My mistake was obvious to me now, for my question had plainly offended him. At a loss what to say, I devoured my simple meal in silence.

After another long inspection of me, the Englishman commenced afresh.

'Do you know Beethoven?'

I replied that I had not yet been to Vienna, but was on my way there to fulfil my dearest wish, to see my beloved master.

'Where do you come from?' he asked.

'From Lembach.'

'That's not very far! I've come from England, also with the

intention of seeing Beethoven. We shall both make his acquaintance; he's a very famous composer.'

What a strange coincidence, I thought to myself. Mighty
master, what diverse kinds thou drawest to thee! On foot and in
carriages they make their journey. This Englishman interested
me; but I swear I did not envy him his carriage. To me it
seemed as though my weary pilgrimage on foot were holier and
more devout, and must render me more blessed than this proud
gentleman who drove there in full state.

Then the postilion blew his horn, and the Englishman drove
off, shouting back to me that he would see Beethoven before I
did.

I had trudged only a few miles farther, when unexpectedly
I encountered him again. It was on the main road, and one of
the carriage axles had broken. He sat inside in majestic ease, with
his valet mounted up behind him, although the vehicle was all
aslant. I learnt that they were waiting for the return of the
postilion, who had run off to a village some distance away to
fetch a blacksmith. As they had already been waiting a long
time, and as the valet spoke nothing but English, I decided to
set off for the village myself, to hurry up both smith and
postilion. In fact I found the latter in a tavern, where spirits
were relieving him of any particular care about the Englishman.
However, I soon brought him back with the smith to the
damaged carriage, which was shortly mended; the Englishman
promised to announce me to Beethoven – and drove away.

Imagine my surprise when I overtook him again the following day! This time, however, nothing was amiss with the
carriage. Drawn up in the middle of the road, he was tranquilly
reading a book, and seemed quite pleased to see me coming.

'I've been waiting a good many hours for you,' he said, 'as it
suddenly occurred to me that I did wrong in not inviting you to
drive with me to Beethoven. Riding is much better than walking.
Come into the carriage.'

I was astonished again. For a moment I really hesitated, and
thought perhaps to accept his invitation; but I soon remembered

the vow I had made the previous day when I saw the Englishman driving off. I had sworn, whatever happened, to pursue my pilgrimage on foot. I told him this openly. It was now the Englishman's turn to be astonished; he could not understand me. He repeated his offer, saying that he had already waited many hours especially for me, in spite of his late arrival at the inn the previous night after the delay caused by the broken axle. I remained firm, and he drove off, wondering.

Frankly, I felt a secret dislike for him; for I was falling prey to a vague foreboding that this Englishman would cause me serious trouble. Moreover, his reverence for Beethoven, and his proposal to make his acquaintance, seemed to me more the idle whim of a wealthy dilettante than the deep inner need of an enthusiastic soul. Therefore I preferred to avoid him, in case my piety might become polluted by his company.

But, as if my destiny meant to prepare me for the dangerous association with this gentleman into which I was eventually to fall, I met him again on the evening of that same day. His carriage was drawn up outside an inn, and it seemed as though he were still waiting for me, for he sat with his back to the horses, looking down the road in my direction.

'Sir,' he began, 'I have again waited a great many hours for you. Will you drive with me to Beethoven?'

This time my astonishment was mingled with a secret terror. I could only explain this striking obstinacy in his attempt to serve me, by the supposition that the Englishman, having noticed my growing antipathy for him, was determined to thrust himself upon me in order to destroy me. With undisguised annoyance, I once more declined his offer, at which he cried out angrily :

'Goddam it, you really don't care for Beethoven. *I* shall soon see him.' And he flew away at great speed.

And that was really the last time I was to meet this Englishman on my still lengthy journey to Vienna. Finally the end of my pilgrimage was reached, and I found myself in the streets of Vienna. With what feelings I arrived at this Mecca of my faith ! All the toil and hardships of my weary journey were forgotten; I was here within the walls that encircled Beethoven.

I was too deeply moved to be able to think of carrying out my aim at once. True, the first thing I did was to inquire for Beethoven's dwelling, but merely in order to find myself lodgings close by. Almost opposite the house in which the master lived, there happened to be a fairly modest inn. I engaged a small room on the fifth floor, and there began to prepare myself for the greatest event of my life, my visit to Beethoven.

I rested for two days, fasting and praying, but never casting another look at the city itself, and then I plucked up courage to leave my inn and march straight across to the house of marvels. I was told Herr Beethoven was not at home. That suited me quite well; for it gave me time to collect myself afresh. But when four times more throughout the day, the same reply was given me, and with a certain increasing emphasis, I realised that day was an unlucky one for me, and abandoned my visit in gloom.

As I was strolling back to the inn, my Englishman waved his hand to me from a first-floor window, with a certain amount of affability.

'Have you seen Beethoven?' he shouted.

'Not yet; he wasn't in,' I answered, rather vexed at encountering him again. When I got inside the Englishman accosted me on the stairs, and with remarkable friendliness insisted upon my entering his apartment.

'Mein Herr', he said, 'I have seen you go to Beethoven's house five times today. I have been here a good many days, and have taken up my quarters in this villainous hotel so as to be near Beethoven. Believe me, it is most difficult to get a word with him; he appears to be most unsociable. At first I went six times a day to his house, and each time I was turned away. Now I get up very early, and sit at my window till late in the evening, to see when Beethoven goes out. But the gentleman seems never to go out.'

'So you think Beethoven was at home today, as well, and had me sent away?' I cried aghast.

'Absolutely! You and I have both been dismissed. And this is very annoying to me, for I came here to see Beethoven, not Vienna.'

That was very sad news for me. Nevertheless I tried my luck again on the following day; but once more in vain. The gates of heaven were closed against me.

My Englishman, who kept constant watch from his window on my fruitless attempts, had now gained positive information that Beethoven's apartments did not face the street. Though very irritating, he was undoubtedly persistent. My patience, on the contrary, was nearly exhausted, for my situation was more desperate; a week had slipped by and I had not reached my goal, and the returns from my polkas and galops allowed only a very brief stay in Vienna. Little by little I began to despair.

I poured my grief into my landlord's ear. He smiled, and promised to tell me the cause of my ill fortune if I would undertake not to repeat what he said to the Englishman. Naturally, I agreed at once.

'You see,' said the worthy innkeeper, 'quite a number of Englishmen come here, to lie in wait for Herr van Beethoven. This annoys Herr van Beethoven very much, and he is so enraged by the effrontery of these people that he has made it quite impossible for any stranger to gain admittance to him. He's an eccentric gentleman, and one must forgive him. But it's very good business for my inn, which is generally packed with Englishmen, whom the difficulty in getting a word with Herr Beethoven compels to be my guests for longer than they would otherwise choose. However, as you promise not to scare away my customers, I shall try to find a means of smuggling you to Herr Beethoven.'

This was very edifying! I could not reach my goal because I, poor devil, was taken for an Englishman. So, my fears had been justified; the Englishman was the cause of my perdition! At first I thought of quitting the inn, since it was certain that everyone who lodged there was regarded by Beethoven's household as an Englishman, and for that reason I, too, was under the ban. However, the landlord's promise to find me an opportunity

c

of speaking with Beethoven held me back. Meanwhile the Englishman, whom I now detested from the bottom of my heart, had been practising all kinds of intrigues and bribery, all to no avail.

Several more fruitless days slipped by, and the revenue from my polkas was visibly dwindling, when at last the landlord confided to me that I would be sure to see Beethoven if I were to go to a certain beer-garden, which the composer was in the habit of visiting almost every day at the same hour. My mentor also gave me such unmistakable directions as to Beethoven's personal appearance, that I could not fail to recognise him. My spirits revived, and I resolved not to defer my fortune any longer. It was impossible for me to meet Beethoven on his way out, as he always left his house by a back door; so there remained nothing but to set off for the beer-garden.

Alas! I sought the master there in vain on that and the two succeeding days. Finally, on the fourth, as I was returning again to the fateful beer-garden at the stated hour, to my despair I noticed that the Englishman was cautiously and carefully following me at a distance. The wretch, posted at his eternal window, had not failed to notice that I went out every day at a certain time in the same direction. Struck by this, and guessing that I must have found some means of tracking Beethoven, he had decided to reap his profit from my supposed discovery. In fact, he told me as much with the calmest impudence, declaring that he meant to follow me wherever I went. All my efforts to deceive him and make him believe that I was only going to refresh myself in a common beer-garden, far too unfashionable to be frequented by gentlemen of his quality, were in vain: he remained unshaken, and I could only curse my fate. At last I gave up being polite and sought to get rid of him by abuse; but, far from letting it provoke him, he contented himself with giving me a placid smile. His fixed idea was to see Beethoven; nothing else troubled him.

And in truth I was this day, at last, to look on the face of the great Beethoven for the first time. Nothing can depict my emotion, and my fury too, as sitting next to my Englishman, I saw a man approach whose looks and bearing completely answered the description the landlord had given me of Beethoven. The long blue overcoat, the tumbled shock of grey hair; and then the features, the expression on the face, exactly as I had remembered them from portraits. There could be no mistake : at the first glance I had recognised him! With short, quick steps he passed us. I sat, transfixed with awe and veneration.

Nothing of this was lost on the Englishman; with avid eyes he watched the newcomer, who withdrew into the farthest corner of the still deserted garden, gave his order for wine, and remained for a while in an attitude of meditation. My throbbing heart cried out "Tis he!' For several moments I completely forgot my neighbour, and watched with eager eye and speechless delight the man whose genius had been lord of all my thoughts and feelings ever since I had learnt to think and feel. Involuntarily I began muttering to myself, and fell into a sort of monologue, which closed with the only too intelligible words : *'Beethoven, it is thou, then, whom I see?'*

Nothing escaped my dreadful neighbour, who, leaning over to me, had listened with bated breath to my soliloquy. From the depths of my ecstasy I was startled by the words :

'Yes! This gentlemen is Beethoven. Come, let us present ourselves to him at once!'

In utter alarm and irritation, I held the cursed Englishman back by the elbow.

'What are you doing?' I cried, 'Do you want to compromise us in this place? Have you no manners at all?'

'What do you mean?' he answered, 'It's a first-rate opportunity; it won't be easy to find a better one.'

With that he drew a kind of notebook from his pocket, and tried to make straight for the man in the blue overcoat. Beside myself, I clutched the idiot's coat-tails, and thundered at him, 'Have you gone mad?'

This scene had attracted the stranger's attention. He appeared to have formed a painful guess that he was the subject of our agitation, and, hastily emptying his glass, he rose to go. No sooner had the Englishman noticed this, than he tore himself from my grasp with such violence that he left one of his coat-tails in my hand, and threw himself across Beethoven's path. The master sought to avoid him; but the wretched man stepped in front, made an elegant bow in the latest English fashion, and addressed him as follows:

'I have the honour to present myself to the much renowned composer and very estimable gentleman, Herr Beethoven. '

He had no need to add more, for at his very first words, Beethoven, after glancing at me, had sprung to one side and vanished from the beer-garden as fast as lightning. Nevertheless the irrepressible Briton was on the point of running after the fugitive, when I seized his remaining coat-tail in a fury of indignation. Somewhat surprised, he stopped, and bellowed at me:

'Goddam it! This Beethoven is a great man, and no mistake. He's worthy to be an Englishman, and I shall lose no time in making his acquaintance.'

I was speechless. This ghastly adventure had crushed my last hope of ever seeing my heart's fondest wish fulfilled.

It was only too clear to me, in fact, that henceforth any attempt on my part to approach Beethoven in an ordinary way would be completely futile. In the utterly threadbare state of my finances I had only the choice of setting out at once for home, with my labour lost, or taking one final desperate step to achieve my ambition. The first alternative sent a shudder to the very bottom of my soul. Who, so near the doors of the highest shrine, could bear to see them shut for ever without falling into the deepest despair?

Before thus abandoning my soul's salvation, I would venture on one more forlorn hope. But *what* step, what road should I take? For a long time I could think of nothing coherent. Alas! my brain was paralysed; nothing presented itself to my over-wrought imagination, except the memory of what I had suffered when I held the coat-tail of that terrible Englishman in my hand.

Beethoven's sidelong glance at my unhappy self, in this fearful catastrophe, had not escaped me; I knew what that glance had meant : he had taken me for an Englishman !

What was to be done to allay the master's suspicion? Everything depended on my letting him know that I was a simple German soul, poor in earthly goods but rich in heavenly enthusiasm for his genius.

So at last I decided to pour out my heart to him in writing. And this I did. I wrote, briefly narrating the history of my life, how I had become a musician, how I worshipped him, how I had long wished to know him in person, how I had spent two years in making a name as a composer of dance music, how I had embarked upon my pilgrimage, what sufferings the Englishman had brought upon me, and what a terrible plight I now was in. As my heart grew noticeably lighter with this recital of my woes, I began to indulge in a certain tone of familiarity; I wove into my letter quite frank and fairly strong reproaches of the master's unjust treatment of my wretched self. Finally I closed the letter in genuine inspiration. By the time I wrote the address : '*An Herrn Ludwig van Beethoven*', tears of ecstasy were in my eyes. I only stopped to breathe a silent prayer, and then rushed off to deliver the letter with my own hands at Beethoven's house.

I returned to my hotel in the highest spirits. But, by heaven, the dreaded Englishman appeared again before my eyes. From his window he had spied my latest move as well. In my face he had read the joy of hope, and that sufficed to place me in his power once more. He stopped me on the steps with the question : 'Good news? When do we see Beethoven?'

'Never, never!' I cried in despair. '*You* will never see Beethoven again, in all your life. Leave me, wretch, we have nothing in common!'

'We have a great deal in common,' he replied coolly. 'Where is my coat-tail, sir? Who authorised you to forcibly deprive me of it? Don't you know that you are to blame for Beethoven's behaviour to me? How could he think it possible to have anything to do with a gentleman wearing only one coat-tail?'

Furious at having the blame thrown back upon myself, I shouted : 'Sir, your coat-tail shall be restored to you. May you keep it as a shameful memento of how you insulted the great Beethoven, and hurled a poor musician to his doom! Farewell. I hope we never meet again.'

He tried to detain and pacify me, assuring me that he had plenty more coats in the best condition. He only wanted to know when Beethoven meant to receive us. But I rushed upstairs to my fifth-floor attic; there I locked myself in, and waited for Beethoven's answer.

How can I ever describe my feelings when the next hour actually brought me a scrap of music-paper, on which was hurriedly written : 'Excuse me, dear sir, if I beg you not to call on me until tomorrow morning, as I am busy preparing some music for the post today. Tomorrow I shall expect you. Beethoven.'

My first action was to fall on my knees and thank Heaven for this exceptional mercy : my eyes grew dim with fervent tears. At last, however, my feelings found vent in the wildest joy; I sprang up, and danced around my tiny room like a lunatic. I'm not quite sure what sort of dance it was. I only remember that to my utter shame I suddenly became aware that I was whistling one of my polkas to it. This mortifying discovery restored me to my senses. I left my garret, ran downstairs and, drunk with joy, rushed into the streets of Vienna.

My God, my sorrows had made me clean forget that I was in Vienna! How delighted I was with the merry ways of the dwellers in this great capital. I was in a state of exaltation, and saw everything through rose-coloured spectacles. The somewhat shallow sensuousness of the Viennese seemed to me to be spontaneous warmth. Their volatile and none too discriminating love of pleasure I took for frank and natural sensitivity to all things beautiful. I ran my eye down the five theatre posters for that day. Heavens! On one of them I saw : *Fidelio*, an opera by Beethoven.

To the theatre I had to go, however much shrunk were the

profits from my dance music. As I entered the pit, the overture began. It was the revised edition of the opera, which, to the honour of the discriminating public of Vienna, had failed under its earlier title, *Leonora*. I had never yet heard the opera in this its second form. Judge, then, my delight at making here my first acquaintance with the glorious new work! A very young girl played the role of Leonora; but youthful as she was, this singer seemed already attuned to Beethoven's genius. With what radiance, what poetry, what depth, did she portray this extraordinary woman! She was called Wilhelmine Schröder. Hers is the high distinction of having revealed this work of Beethoven to the German-speaking public; for that evening I saw even the superficial Viennese aroused to the strongest enthusiasm. For my own part, the heavens were opened to me; I was transported, and adored the genius who had led me – just as, in his opera, Florestan was led – from night and fetters into light and freedom.

I could not sleep that night. What I had just experienced, and what was in store for me next day, were too great and overpowering for me to succumb to sleep and dreams. I lay awake, building castles in the air and preparing myself for Beethoven's presence. At last the new day dawned; impatiently I waited till the proper hour for a morning visit. Eventually, I set forth. The weightiest event of my life stood before me: I trembled at the thought.

However, I had still one fearful trial to pass through.

Leaning against the wall of Beethoven's house, as cool as a cucumber, my evil spirit waited for me – the Englishman! The monster, after suborning all the world, had ended by bribing our landlord, who had read the open note from Beethoven before myself, and betrayed its contents to the Briton.

A cold sweat came over me at the sight. All my excitement, all my heavenly exaltation vanished; once more I was in *his* power.

'Come,' began the villain, 'let us introduce ourselves to Beethoven.'

At first I thought of getting out of the situation by lying, and pretending that I was not about to visit Beethoven at all. But he cut the ground from under my feet by telling me with the greatest candour how he had got to the bottom of my secret, and declared that he had no intention of leaving me till we both returned from the visit. I tried soft words, to move him from his purpose – in vain! I flew into a rage – in vain! At last I attempted to outwit him by fleetness of foot. Swift as an arrow I darted up the steps, and tore at the bell like a maniac. But before the door was opened the gentleman was by my side, tugging at the tail of my coat and saying: 'You can't escape me. I've a right to your coat-tail, and I shall hold on to it until we are in Beethoven's presence.'

Infuriated, I turned round and tried to tear myself free. Indeed, I felt tempted to defend myself against this insolent son of Britain by deeds of violence. But then the door was opened. The old serving-maid appeared, made a wry face at the odd picture we presented, and promptly began to shut the door again. In my agony I shouted out my name, and protested that I had been invited by Herr Beethoven himself.

The old lady was still hesitating, for the look of the Englishman seemed to fill her with a proper apprehension, when Beethoven himself, as luck would have it, appeared at the door of his study. Seizing the opportunity, I stepped quickly in, and moved towards the master to tender my apologies. At the same time, however, I inadvertently dragged the Englishman behind me, as he was still holding me tight. He carried out his threat, and never released me till we were both standing before Beethoven. I made my bow, and stammered out my name. Although, of course, he did not hear it, the master seemed to guess that it was I who had written to him. He bade me enter his room. Without paying any attention to Beethoven's astonished glance, my companion slipped in after me.

Here I was in the sanctuary, and yet the state of hideous confusion into which the awful Briton had plunged me robbed me of all that sense of well-being so requisite for due enjoyment of my fortune. Nor was Beethoven's outward appearance at all calculated to fill one with a sense of ease. He was clad in somewhat untidy house-clothes, with a red woollen scarf wrapped round his waist. Long, bushy grey hair hung in disorder from his head, and his gloomy, forbidding expression was far from reassuring. We took our seats at a table strewn with pens and paper.

An uncomfortable feeling held us tongue-tied. It was only too evident that Beethoven was displeased at receiving two people instead of one.

At last he began, in grating tones: 'You come from Lembach?' I was about to reply, when he stopped me. Passing me a sheet of paper and a pencil, he added: 'Please write. I cannot hear.'

I knew of Beethoven's deafness, and had prepared myself for it. Nevertheless it was like a stab through my heart when I heard his hoarse and broken words, 'I cannot hear'. To stand joyless and poor in the world, to be uplifted by nothing but the power of music, and then to be forced to say, 'I cannot hear'! That moment gave me the key to Beethoven's exterior, the deep furrows on his cheeks, the sombre dejection of his look, the set defiance of his lips. He could not hear!

Distraught, and scarcely knowing what I was doing, I wrote down an apology, with a brief account of the circumstances that had made me appear in the Englishman's company. Meanwhile the latter sat silently and calmly contemplating Beethoven, who, as soon as he had read my note, turned rather sharply to him and asked what he wanted.

'I have the honour – ' commenced the Briton.

'I don't understand you!' cried Beethoven, hastily interrupting him; 'I cannot hear, nor can I speak much. Please write down what you want of me.'

The Englishman placidly reflected for a moment, then drew an elaborate music-case from his pocket, and said to me: 'Very well. Please write: "I beg Herr Beethoven to look through my composition; if any passage does not please him, will he have the kindness to set a cross against it." '

I wrote down his request, word for word, in the hope of getting rid of him at last. And so it happened. After Beethoven had read my note, he laid the Englishman's composition on the table with a peculiar smile, nodded his head, and said, 'I will send it back to you.'

With this my gentleman was extremely pleased; he rose, made an especially elegant bow, and took his leave. I drew a deep breath: he was gone.

Now for the first time did I really feel myself within the sanctuary. Even Beethoven's features visibly brightened. He looked at me quietly for an instant, then began: 'The Briton has caused you much annoyance? Take comfort from me. These travelling Englishmen have plagued me almost out of my wits. Today they come to stare at a poor musician, tomorrow at a rare wild beast. I am truly grieved at having confused you with them. You wrote that you liked my compositions. I'm glad of that, for nowadays I hardly expect people to be pleased with my things.'

This confidential tone soon removed my last embarrassment, and a thrill of joy ran through me at these simple words. I wrote that I certainly was not the only one imbued with such glowing enthusiasm for every creation of his, that I wished for nothing more ardently than to be able to secure for my home town, for instance, the happiness of receiving him. Then he would be convinced of the impression his works produced on the entire public there.

'I can quite believe,' answered Beethoven, 'that my compositions find more favour in Northern Germany. The Viennese frequently annoy me. They hear too much poor stuff each day, to be able to take good music seriously.'

I ventured to dispute this, mentioning the performance of *Fidelio* I had attended on the previous evening, which the Viennese public had greeted with the most demonstrative enthusiasm.

'H'm, h'm!' muttered the master. '*Fidelio*! But I know the silly creatures are clapping their hands today out of pure conceit, for they fancy that in revising this opera I merely followed their own advice. So they want to pay me for my trouble, and cry bravo! They're good-natured people though none too learned; I would rather be with them I suppose, than with sober people. Do you like *Fidelio*, then?'

I described the impression made on me by the previous evening's performance, and remarked that the entire work had gained enormously by the pieces he had added to it.

'Irksome work!' rejoined Beethoven. 'I am no opera-composer; at least, I can't think of any theatre in the world for which I should care to write another opera! If I were to write an opera after my own heart, everyone would run away from it; for it would have none of your arias, duets, trios, and all the stuff they patch up operas with today. What I should set in their place no singer would sing, and no audience listen to. They all know nothing but gaudy lies, glittering nonsense, and sugared tedium. Whoever wrote a true musical drama, would be taken for a fool; and so indeed he would be, if he didn't keep such a thing to himself, but wanted to present it before an audience.'

'How does one set about composing such a musical drama?' I asked.

'The same way as Shakespeare did, when he wrote his plays,' was the almost passionate answer. 'Whoever concocts all kinds of pretty things with which ladies with passable voices may earn *bravi* and hand-claps, had better become a Parisian lady's-tailor, not a dramatic composer. For my part, I was never made for such idiocy. Oh, I know quite well that the clever say I am good enough at instrumental music, but should never be at home in vocal. They are perfectly right, since vocal music for them means nothing but operatic music. May the gods preserve me from being at home in that nonsense!'

I ventured to ask whether he really believed that anyone, after hearing his song *Adelaide*, would dare to deny that he was a most brilliant composer of vocal music.

'Ah!' he replied after a little pause, '*Adelaide* and the like are only trifles after all, and they are useful enough to professional virtuosi as a fresh opportunity for letting off their fireworks. But why should not vocal music, as much as instrumental, form a grand and serious genre, and its execution meet with as much respect from the feather-brained warblers as I demand from an orchestra for one of my symphonies? The human voice is not to be gainsaid. No, it is a far more beautiful and noble organ of sound than any instrument in the orchestra. If only one could employ it with just the same freedom as these. What entirely new results one would gain from such a procedure! For the very timbre that naturally distinguishes the voice of man from the mechanical instrument would have to be given especial prominence, and that would lead to the most varied combinations. The instruments represent the rudimentary organs of Creation and Nature. What they express can never be clearly defined or put into words, for they reproduce the primitive feelings themselves, those feelings which issued from the chaos of the first Creation, when perhaps there was not as yet a single human being to take them up into his heart. It's quite otherwise with the genius of the human voice. The voice represents the heart of man and its well-defined individual emotion. Its character is consequently restricted, but definite and clear. Now, let us bring these two elements together, and unite them! Let us set the wild, unfettered elemental feelings, represented by the instruments, in contact with the clear and definite emotion of the human heart, as represented by the voice of man. The advent of this second element will calm and smooth the conflict of those primal feelings, will give their waves a definite, united course; whilst the human heart itself, absorbing those primordial feelings, will be immeasurably strengthened and widened, equipped to feel with perfect clearness its earlier indefinite presage of the Highest, transformed thereby to godlike consciousness.'

Here Beethoven paused for a few moments, as if exhausted. Then he continued with a gentle sigh : 'To be sure, in the attempt to solve this problem one lights on many obstacles; to make men sing, one must give them words. Yet who could frame in words that sublime poetry needed to form the basis of such a union of all the elements? The poem must necessarily limp behind, for words are vehicles too weak for such a task. You will soon make the acquaintance of a new composition of mine, which will remind you of what I have just touched on. It is a symphony with choruses in its final movement. When you hear it, consider how hard I found it to disguise the shortcomings of poetry. At last I decided to use Schiller's beautiful *Ode to Joy*. It is certainly a noble and inspiring poem, yet it does not perfectly express that which, certainly in this connection, no verses in the world could convey.'

To this day I can scarcely believe my happiness at thus being helped by Beethoven himself to a full understanding of his gigantic Ninth Symphony, which at that time was almost finished, but known as yet to no one. I thanked him fervently for this rare condescension. At the same time I expressed what a delightful surprise it had been to me to hear that we might look forward to the appearance of a new great work composed by him. Tears had welled into my eyes. I could have gone down on my knees to him.

Beethoven seemed to notice my agitation. Half sadly, half roguishly, he looked into my face and said : 'You might care to take my part, when my new work is discussed. Remember me : for the clever ones will think I am out of my senses. At least, that is what they will say. But perhaps you will realise that I am not quite mad yet, though unhappy enough to become so. People want me to write according to *their* ideas of what is good and beautiful; they never reflect that I, a poor deaf man, must have my own ideas, that it would be impossible for me to write otherwise than as I feel. That I cannot think and feel by their standards,' he added in irony, 'is just my misfortune !'

With that he rose, and paced the room with short, quick steps. Stirred to my inmost heart as I was, I stood up too. I could feel myself trembling. It would have been impossible for me to continue the conversation either by gesture or writing. I was conscious also that the point had been reached when my visit might become a burden to the master. To *write* a farewell word of heartfelt thanks, seemed too matter-of-fact; so I contented myself with seizing my hat, approaching Beethoven, and letting him read in my eyes what was passing within me.

He seemed to understand. 'You are going?' he asked. 'Will you remain in Vienna awhile?'

I wrote that my journey had no other object than to gain his personal acquaintance. Since he had honoured me with so unique a reception, I was overjoyed to view my goal as reached, and should start for home again next day.

Smiling, he replied: 'You wrote how you had procured the money for this journey. You ought to stop in Vienna and write dance music. That sort of thing is greatly valued here.'

I declared that I had done with all that, as I now knew nothing worth a similar sacrifice.

'Well, well,' he said, 'one never knows! Old fool that I am, I should have done better, myself, to write galops and polkas. As it is, I shall always be poor. Have a pleasant journey,' he added. 'Think of me, and let that console you in all your troubles.'

My eyes full of tears, I was about to withdraw, when he called to me: 'One moment, we must polish off the musical Englishman! Let's see where to put the crosses!'

He snatched up the Briton's music-case, and smilingly skimmed its contents. Then he carefully put it in order again, wrapped it in a sheet of paper, took a broad-nibbed pen, and drew a huge cross from one end of the cover to the other. Whereupon he handed it to me with the words: 'Kindly give the happy man his masterpiece! He's a fool and yet I envy him his folly! Farewell, dear friend, and continue to think well of me!'

And so he dismissed me. With staggering steps I left his room, and the house.

At the hotel I found the Englishman's servant packing his master's trunks into the carriage. So his goal, also, was reached; I had to admit that he, too, had proved his endurance. I ran up to my room, and likewise made ready to commence my homeward march on the morrow. A fit of laughter seized me when I looked at the cross on the cover of the Englishman's composition. That cross, however, was a souvenir of Beethoven, and I grudged it to the evil genius of my pilgrimage. My decision was quickly taken. I removed the cover, hunted out my galops and polkas, and clapped them in this damning shroud. I returned the Englishman's composition wrapperless, accompanying it with a little note in which I told him that Beethoven envied him and had declared he didn't know where to set a cross.

As I was leaving the inn, I saw my wretched comrade mount into his carriage.

'Goodbye,' he cried. 'You have done me a great service. I am glad to have made Beethoven's acquaintance. Will you come with me to Italy?'

'Why are you going there?' I asked in reply.

'I wish to know Mr Rossini, as he is a very famous composer.'

'Good luck!' I called. 'I know Beethoven, and that's enough for a lifetime!'

We parted. I cast one longing glance at Beethoven's house, and turned to the north, uplifted in heart, and ennobled.

A Happy Evening

See introductory note to *A Pilgrimage to Beethoven*.

*

It was a fine spring evening. The heat of summer had already begun to announce itself with delicious breezes that thronged the air like sighs of love and fired our senses. We had followed the stream of people pouring towards a public garden, for here an excellent orchestra was to give the first of its annual series of summer evening concerts. It was a red-letter day. My friend Robert, who was later to die in Paris, was in the seventh heaven of delight. Even before the concert began, he was drunk with music: he said inner harmonies always sang and rang within him when he felt the happiness of a beautiful spring evening.

We arrived, and took our usual places at a table beneath a great oak-tree, for careful comparison had taught us not only that this spot was farthest from the buzzing crowd, but also that here one heard the music most clearly and distinctly. We had always pitied the poor creatures who were compelled, or actually preferred to stay in the immediate vicinity of the orchestra, whether in or out of doors; we could never understand how they found any pleasure in seeing music, instead of hearing it; and yet we could not otherwise account for their rapt attention to the various movements of the band, their enthusiastic interest in the kettle-drummer when, after an anxious counting of his bars of rest, he came in at last with a rousing stroke. We were agreed that nothing can be more prosaic and upsetting, than the hideous aspect of the swollen cheeks and puckered features of the wind-players, the unaesthetic grabbings of the double-bass and 'cellos, indeed even the wearisome sawing of the violin-bows, when one is trying to listen to the performance of fine instrumental music. For this reason we had taken our seats where we could hear the lightest nuance of the orchestra, without being pained by its appearance.

The concert began. Great things were played : among others, Mozart's Symphony in E flat, and Beethoven's in A.

The concert was over. Dumb, but delighted and smiling, my friend sat facing me with folded arms. The crowd departed, group by group, with pleasant chatter; here and there a few tables were still occupied. The evening's genial warmth began to yield to the colder breath of night.

'Let's have some punch!' cried Robert, suddenly turning round to look for a waiter.

Moods like that in which we found ourselves, are too precious not to be maintained for as long as possible. I knew how comforting the punch would be, and eagerly concurred with my friend's proposition. A decent sized bowl was soon steaming on our table, and we emptied our first glasses.

'How did you like the performance of the symphonies?' I asked.

'Oh, the performance?' exclaimed Robert. 'There are moods in which, however critical one may be at other times, the worst execution of one of my favourite works would transport me. These moods, it's true, are rare, and only exercise their sweet dominion over me when my whole inner being stands in blissful harmony with my state of bodily health. Then it needs but the faintest intimation for me to experience at once the whole piece that appeals to my sensibilities; and in so ideal a way that the best orchestra in the world could never bring it to my outward hearing so successfully. In such moods my otherwise very scrupulous musical ear is complaisant enough to allow even the quack of an oboe to cause me but a momentary twinge; with an indulgent smile I let the false note of a trumpet graze my ear, without being torn from the blessed feeling that cheats me into the belief that I am hearing the most consummate execution of my favourite work. In such a mood, nothing irritates me more than to see a well-groomed dandy voicing his well-bred indignation at one of those musical slips that wound his pampered ear, when I know that tomorrow he will be applauding the most excruciating scale with which some popular prima donna does violence to both nerves and soul. Music merely ambles past the ear of these super-subtle fools; indeed often merely past their eye: for I remember noticing people who never stirred a muscle when a brass instrument really went wrong, but put their hands over their ears the instant they saw the wretched player shake his head in shame and confusion.'

'What?' I interposed, 'are you really complaining about people of sensitive ear? How often have I seen you raging like a madman at the faulty intonation of a singer?'

'My friend,' cried Robert, 'I was simply speaking of the present, of tonight. God knows how often I have been nearly driven mad by the mistakes of a famous violinist; how often I have cursed the most renowned of prima donnas when she thought her tone so pure, though she was vocalising somewhere between the notes. How often have I been unable to find the smallest consonance among the instruments of the very best-tuned orchestra. But that is on the countless days when my good angel has deserted me, when I put on my Sunday coat and squeeze between the perfumed ladies and elegant gentlemen to try to entice happiness back into my soul through these ears of mine. Oh, you should feel the pains with which I then weigh every note and measure each vibration! When my heart is dumb, I'm as subtle as any of the prigs who vexed me today, and there are hours when a Beethoven sonata with violin or 'cello will put me to flight. Blessed be the god who made the spring and music: tonight I'm happy.' With that he filled our glasses again, and we drained them to the dregs.

'Need I say,' I began in turn, 'that I feel as happy as yourself?

Who would not be, after listening in peace and comfort to the performance of two works which seem created by the very god of high aesthetic joy? I thought the conjunction of the Mozart and the Beethoven symphonies a most apt idea; I seemed to find a marked relationship between the two compositions; in both, the clear human consciousness that man should rejoice in his life is beautifully transfigured by the presentiment of a higher world beyond. The only distinction I would make, is that in Mozart's music the language of the heart is shaped to graceful longing, whereas in Beethoven's conception this longing reaches out a bolder hand to seize the infinite. In Mozart's symphony the full-ness of feeling predominates, in Beethoven's the manly conscious-ness of strength.'

'It does me good to hear such views expressed about the character and meaning of these sublime instrumental works,' replied my friend. 'Not that I believe you have anything like exhausted their nature with your brief description; but to get to the bottom of that, to say nothing of defining it, lies just as little within the power of human speech as it resides in the nature of music to express in clear and definite terms what can be expressed only by poetry. It's a great misfortune that so many people take the useless trouble to confuse the language of music and that of poetry, and endeavour to make good or replace by the one what in their narrow minds remains imperfect in the other. It is an eternal truth that, where the speech of man stops short, there the art of music begins. Nothing is more intolerable than the mawkish scenes and anecdotes people foist upon some instrumental works. What poverty of mind and feeling it betrays, when the listener to a performance of one of Beethoven's sym-phonies has to keep his interest awake by imagining that the torrent of musical sounds is meant to reproduce the plot of some romance! These people then presume to grumble at the great composer, when an unexpected stroke disturbs the even tenor of their little tale; they tax the composer with unclearness and inconsequence, and deplore his lack of continuity! The idiots!'

'Never mind!' said I. 'Let each man conjure scenes and

fancies according to the strength of his imagination; by their aid perhaps he acquires a taste for these great musical revelations, which many would be quite unable to enjoy for themselves. At least you must admit that the number of Beethoven's admirers has increased this way. It is to be hoped the great musician's works will thereby reach a popularity they could never have attained if they could be only understood in an ideal manner.'

'Merciful Heavens!' Robert exclaimed. 'Even for these sublime works of art you would seek banal popularity, the curse of every grand and noble thing? Perhaps you would also suggest that they should be honoured because their inspiring rhythms can be used to dance to in a village tavern?'

'You exaggerate,' I answered calmly. 'I do not claim for Beethoven's symphonies the popularity of street and tavern. But would you not count it a greater merit if they were in a position to give a gladder impulse to the cribbed and confined heart of the ordinary man in the street?'

'They shall have no merit, these symphonies!' my friend replied, in a huff. 'They exist for themselves and their own sake, not to improve the circulation of a philistine's blood. Let those who are capable of understanding those revelations, do so. Masterpieces are not obliged to force themselves upon the understanding of indifferent hearts.'

I filled my glass, and exclaimed with a laugh: 'You're the same old idealist, who declines to understand me on the very point on which at heart we agree! So let's drop this question of popularity. But give me the pleasure of learning your own sensations when you heard the two symphonies tonight.'

Like a passing cloud the irritation cleared from my friend's lowered brow. He watched the steam ascending from our punch, and smiled. 'My sensations? I felt the soft warmth of a lovely spring evening, and I imagined I was sitting with you beneath a great oak and looking up between its branches to the star-strewn heavens. I felt a thousand other things as well, but they are impossible to communicate. There you have it all.'

'Not bad!' I remarked. 'Perhaps one of our neighbours

imagined he was smoking a cigar, drinking coffee, and making eyes at a young lady in a blue dress.'

'Without a doubt,' Robert continued with sarcasm, 'and the drummer apparently thought he was beating his ill-behaved children, for not having brought him his supper from home. Capital! At the gate I saw a peasant listening in wonder and delight to the Symphony in A: I would wager all I have that he understood it best of all, for you will have read in one of our musical journals a short while ago that what Beethoven had in mind when he composed this symphony, was a description of a peasant's wedding. The honest rustic will thus have remembered his own wedding-day, and revived its every incident: the guests' arrival and the feast, the march to the church, the blessing, the dance, and finally the crowning joy that bride and bridegroom shared alone.'

'A good idea!' I cried, when I had finished laughing. 'But for heaven's sake tell me why you want to prevent this symphony from affording the good peasant his own kind of happiness? Did he not feel, in his own way, the same delight as yourself when you sat beneath the oak and watched the stars of heaven through its branches?'

'There I am with you,' my friend complacently replied. 'I would gladly let the worthy yokel recall his wedding-day when listening to the Symphony in A. But as for the civilised townsfolk who write in musical journals, I should like to tear the hair from their stupid heads when they foist such fudge on honest people, and rob them of all the simplicity with which they would otherwise have settled down to hear Beethoven's symphony. Instead of abandoning themselves to their natural sensations, the poor deluded people with their good hearts but feeble brains feel obliged to look out for a peasant's wedding, a thing they probably have never attended. They would do far better to imagine something within their own experience instead.'

'So you agree with me,' I said, 'that the nature of those creations does not prevent their being variously interpreted, according to the individual?'

'On the contrary,' was the answer, 'I consider a stereotyped interpretation altogether inadmissible. Just as the musical fabric of a Beethoven symphony stands rounded and complete in all its artistic proportions, perfect and indivisible as it appears to the higher sense, so it is impossible to reduce its effects on the human heart to one authoritative type. This is more or less the case with the creations of every other art : how differently will one and the same picture or drama affect two different human beings, or even the heart of one and the same individual at different times! Yet how much more definitely and sharply the painter or poet is bound to draw his figures, than the instrumental composer who, unlike him, is not compelled to model his shapes by the features of the daily world, but has a boundless realm at his disposal in the kingdom of the supermundane, and to whom is given the most spiritual of substances – that of sound! One would be dragging the musician from this high estate, if one tried to make him fit his inspiration to the semblance of that everyday world; and furthermore the instrumental composer would betray his calling, or expose his weakness, if he were to aim at carrying the cramped proportions of purely worldly things into the province of his art.'

'So you reject all tone-painting?' I asked.

'Absolutely,' answered Robert. 'Except where it is employed either in jest or reproduces purely musical phenomena. When it is a question of jest, anything is permissible, for its nature is a certain intended eccentricity, and to laugh and let others laugh is a splendid thing. But where tone-painting leaves this region, it becomes absurd. The inspirations and incitements to an in-strumental composition must be of such a kind that they can arise only in the soul of a musician.'

'You have just said something you will have difficulty in proving,' I objected. 'At heart, I agree with you; but I doubt if all this is quite compatible with our unqualified admiration for the works of our great masters. Don't you think that this maxim of yours flatly contradicts a part of Beethoven's reve-lations?'

'Not in the slightest. On the contrary, I hope to found my proof on Beethoven.'

'Before we get down to details,' I continued, 'don't you feel that Mozart's conception of instrumental music corresponds far better with your assertion, than that of Beethoven?'

'I'm not aware of it,' replied my friend. 'Beethoven immensely enlarged the form of the symphony when he discarded the proportions of the older musical period, which had attained their utmost beauty in Mozart, and followed his impatient genius with bolder but ever more conclusive freedom to regions where he alone could venture. As he also knew how to give these soaring flights a philosophical coherence, it is undeniable that upon the basis of the Mozart symphony he reared a wholly new artistic genre, which he at the same time perfected in every point. But Beethoven would have been unable to achieve all this, had Mozart not previously addressed his conquering genius to the symphony also; had his animating, idealising breath not given a spiritual warmth to the soulless forms and diagrams accepted up till then. It is from this point that Beethoven departed and the artist who had taken Mozart's divinely pure soul unto himself could never descend from that high altitude which is true music's sole domain.'

'By all means,' I resumed. 'You will hardly deny, however, that Mozart's music flowed from none but a musical source, that his inspiration started from an indefinite inner feeling, which, even had he had a poet's faculty, could never have been conveyed in words, but always and exclusively in notes. I am speaking of those inspirations which arise in the musician simultaneously with his melodies, with his notation. Mozart's music bears the characteristic stamp of this instantaneous birth, and it is impossible to suppose that he would ever have drafted the plan of a symphony, for instance, without having all the themes, and in fact the entire structure as we know it, already in his head. On the other hand, I cannot help thinking that Beethoven planned the order of a symphony according to a certain philosophical idea, before he left it to his imagination to invent the musical themes.'

'And how do you propose to prove that?' my friend ejaculated.
'By this evening's symphony perhaps?'

'That might be difficult,' I answered, 'but is it not enough simply to mention the "Eroica" symphony, in support of my contention? You know, of course, that this symphony was originally meant to bear the title "Bonaparte". Can you deny, then, that Beethoven was inspired and prompted to plan this giant work by an idea outside the realm of music?'

'I'm delighted at your mentioning that symphony!' Robert quickly put in. 'You surely don't mean to say that the idea of a heroic force reaching violently towards the highest, is outside the realm of music? Or do you find that Beethoven has translated his enthusiasm for the victorious young conqueror into petty details which make you think he intended this symphony as a musical bulletin of the first Italian campaign?'

'What do you mean?' I interposed. 'Have I said anything of the sort?'

'It's at the back of your contention,' my friend went on passionately. 'If we are to assume that Beethoven sat down to write a composition in honour of Bonaparte, we must also conclude that he would have been unable to turn out anything but one of those "occasional" pieces which are all still-born. But the *Sinfonia eroica* is an entire world away from anything of that kind. No: had the master set himself a task like that, he would have fulfilled it most unsatisfactorily. Tell me, where, in what part of this composition do you find one positive hint that the composer had his eye on a specific event in the heroic career of the young commander? What do the Funeral March, the Scherzo with the hunting-horns, the Finale with the soft emotional Andante mean? Where is the Bridge of Lodi, where is the Battle of Arcole, where is the victory under the Pyramids, where is the 18 Brumaire?[1] Are these not incidents which no composer of

---

[1] The coup d'état of 18 Brumaire, year VIII (9th November, 1799), with the law of 19 Brumaire, overthrew the Directory and established the consular regime.

our day would have allowed to escape him, if he wanted to write a biographical symphony on Bonaparte? Here, however, this was not the case; and permit me to tell you my own idea of the gestation of this symphony. When a musician feels prompted to sketch the smallest composition, he is moved by a powerful feeling which overwhelms his whole being at the hour of conception. This mood may be brought about by an outward experience, or it may have risen from a secret inner source. Whether it be melancholy, joy, desire, contentment, love or hatred, in the musician it will always take a musical shape, and manifest itself in notes. But grand, passionate and lasting emotions, dominating all our feelings and ideas for months and often half a year, drive the musician to those vaster, more intense conceptions to which we owe, among others, the origin of a *Sinfonia eroica*. These greater moods, such as deep suffering of the soul or potent exaltation, may spring from outside events, for we are all men, and our fate is ruled by outward circumstances. But when they force the musician to production, these greater moods have already turned to music in him, so that at the moment of creative inspiration it is no longer the outside event that governs the composer, but the musical sensation which it has begotten in him. Now, what phenomenon is worthier to rouse and keep alive the sympathy, the inspiration of a genius so full of fire as Beethoven, than that of the youthful conqueror who rased a world in order to mould a new one from its ruins? Imagine the musician following from deed to deed, from victory to victory, the man who impelled friend and foe alike to admiration! And the republican Beethoven, to boot, who looked to that hero for the realisation of his ideal dreams of universal human good! How his blood must have surged, his heart glowed, when that glorious name rang back to him wherever he turned to commune with his Muse! He must have felt incited to a similar magnificent sweep; his will to victory must have been spurred on to a like deed of untold grandeur. He was no general, he was a musician; and in his domain he saw the way in which he could bring to pass a triumph equal to that of Bonaparte in the plains

of Italy. His musical force at its highest strength bade him conceive a work the like of which had never before been dreamt
of. He brought forth his *Sinfonia eroica*, and knowing well to
whom he owed the impulse to this gigantic work, he wrote upon
its title-page the name of Bonaparte. And in fact is not this
symphony as clear a proof of man's creative power, as Bonaparte's glorious victory? Yet, I ask you, is there a single trait
in its development that has an immediate outer connection with
the fate of the hero, who at that time had not even reached
the zenith of his destined fame? I am happy enough to admire
in it nothing but a gigantic monument of art, to fortify myself by
the strength and joyous exaltation which swell my breast on
hearing it; and to leave more learned folk to spell out the Battles
of Rivoli and Marengo from its score's mysterious hieroglyphs!'

The night air had grown colder. During this speech, a passing
waiter had taken my hint to remove the punch and warm it up
again. He now came back, and once more the grateful beverage
was steaming high before our eyes. I filled my glass, and held out
my hand to Robert.

'We are in agreement,' I said, 'as always where innermost
questions of art are concerned. Whatever our mood, we shouldn't
deserve the name of musicians, if we could fall into such blatant
errors about the nature of our art as you have just denounced.
What music expresses is eternal, infinite, and ideal. She expresses
not the passion, love, desire of this or that individual in this or
that condition, but Passion, Love, Desire itself, and in such
infinitely varied phases as belong uniquely to music and which
are foreign and unknown to any other tongue. Let each man
taste of her according to his strength, his faculty and mood,
whatever he has the power to taste!'

'And tonight,' my friend broke in, full of enthusiasm, 'it's joy
I taste, the happiness, the presage of a higher destiny, won from
the wondrous revelations in which Mozart and Beethoven have
spoken to us on this glorious spring evening. So here's to
happiness, to joy! Here's to courage, that heartens us when we
battle with our fate! Here's to victory, gained by our higher

sense over the worthlessness of the vulgar! To love, which crowns our courage; to friendship, that keeps firm our faith! To hope, which weds itself to our foreboding! To the day, to the night! A cheer for the sun, a cheer for the stars! And three cheers for music and her high priests! May God be adored and worshipped for ever, the God of joy and happiness, the God who created music! Amen.'

Arm-in-arm we wended our way homewards. We pressed each other's hand, and not another word did we say.

An End in Paris

See introductory note to *A Pilgrimage to Beethoven*.

*

We have just laid Robert in the earth. It was cold and dreary weather, and there were only a few of us. The Englishman, too, was there. He wants to erect a memorial to him; he could more usefully pay our friend's debts.

It was a mournful ceremony. The first keen wind of winter cut to the quick; no one could speak, and the funeral oration was omitted. Nevertheless I would have you know that he whom we buried was a good man and a brave German musician. He had a tender heart, and wept whenever men hit the poor horses in the streets of Paris. He was mild of temper, and was never put out when street-urchins jostled him off the narrow pavement. Unfortunately he had a sensitive artistic conscience, and was ambitious, with no talent for intrigue. Once in his youth he had seen Beethoven, which so turned his head that he could never set it straight again.

It is more than a year since I saw a magnificent Newfoundland dog taking a bath one day in the fountain of the Palais Royal. Lover of dogs that I am, I watched the splendid animal. Eventually it left the basin and answered the call of a man who at first attracted my attention merely because he was the owner of this dog. The man was by no means as attractive as his dog. He was clean, but dressed in a most provincial fashion.

Yet his features arrested me. Soon I distinctly remembered where I had seen them before, and my interest in the dog waned : I fell into the arms of my old friend Robert.

We were delighted at meeting again, and he was quite over-come with emotion. I took him to the Café de la Rotonde; I drank tea with rum, and he, coffee with tears.

'But what on earth,' I began at last, 'can have brought you to Paris? You, musical hermit of a provincial back-street attic?'

'My friend,' he replied, 'call it the over-zealous passion for experiencing what life is like in a Parisian sixth-floor garret, or the worldly longing to see if I might not be able in time to afford the second, or even the first floor. At any rate I couldn't resist the temptation to tear myself away from the squalor of the German provinces, and, without tasting the far sublimer delights of a German capital, to throw myself at the centre of the world, where the arts of every nation stream together in unison; where the artists of every race find recognition; and where I hope to satisfy the tiny morsel of ambition that Heaven, apparently in inadvertence, has set in my own breast.'

'A very natural desire,' I interposed. 'I forgive you, though that you should feel so astonishes me. But first tell me what means you have of pursuing your ambitious purpose. How much money per year can you count on? Oh, don't be alarmed! I know that you are not well off, and it is self-evident that there can be no question of a settled income. Yet I am bound to suppose either that you have won money in a lottery, or that you enjoy the protection of some rich patron or relative to such a degree that you are provided with a passable allowance for at least ten years.'

'That is how you foolish people look at things!' replied my friend, with a good-humoured smile, after recovering from his first alarm. 'Such are the prosaic details that occur to you im-mediately as the chief concern. Nothing of the kind, my dear friend! I am poor. In a few weeks, in fact, I shan't have a sou left. But what of that? I have been told that I have talent. Was I to choose Tunis as the place for pushing it? No, I have come to Paris! Here I shall soon find out if people deceived me when they credited me with talent, or if I really have any. In the first case I shall be quickly disenchanted, and, with no illusions about myself, shall journey home contentedly to my attic. In the second case I shall have my talent more speedily and warmly recognised in Paris, than anywhere else in the world. No, don't smile, but try to raise some serious objection!'

'Dear friend,' I resumed, 'I smile no longer; for now I am possessed by a mournful compassion for both you and your splendid dog. I know that, however frugal you may be yourself, your magnificent beast will need to eat a good deal. Do you intend to feed both him and yourself by your talent? That's wonderful, for self-preservation is man's first duty, and human feeling for all beasts his second and most noble task. But, tell me, how are you going to put your talent on the market? What plans have you made? Let me hear them.'

'I am glad that you ask me about my plans,' he replied. 'You shall have a long list of them, for I assure you I am rich in plans. In the first place, I'm thinking of an opera, in fact, I have finished works, half-finished works, and any number of sketches of all kinds, for both grand and comic opera. Don't interrupt! I'm well aware that these are things that will not sell too quickly, and I consider them merely as the basis of my efforts. Though I dare not hope to see one of my operas produced at once, at least I may be permitted to assume that I shall soon be satisfied as to whether the Directors will accept my compositions or not. Now, really, my friend, you're smiling again! Don't speak! I know what you are going to say, and will answer it at once. I am convinced that I shall have to contend with difficulties of all sorts here in Paris; but in what will they consist? There will be competition, certainly. The most eminent talents converge here, and offer their works for acceptance. Managers are therefore compelled to exercise a searching scrutiny: a cross must be marked against the work of bunglers, and only works of exceptional merit can attain the honour of selection. Good! I have prepared myself for this scrutiny, and ask for no distinction which I have not won. But what else have I to fear, besides competition?

Am I to believe that here, too, one must employ the usual tactics
of servility? Here in Paris, the capital of free France, where a
press exists that unmasks and makes impossible all humbug and
abuse, where merit alone can win the plaudits of a great in-
corruptible public?'

'The public?' I interrupted. 'There you are right. I also am
of the opinion that, with your talent, you might well succeed,
if you had only the public to contend with. But, as to the ease
with which you may contact that public, you greatly err, my
poor friend! It is not a battle of talents in which you will have
to engage, but a battle of reputations and personal interests. If
you are sure of firm and influential patronage, by all means
venture into the fight; but without this, and without money, give
up, for you're sure to go under, without so much as being noticed.
It is not your work or your talent that will be considered, but
only the name you bear. As no renown attaches to that name as
yet, and it is not to be found on a list of the moneyed, you and
your talent must remain in obscurity.'

My objection failed to produce the intended effect on my
enthusiastic friend. He turned peevish, and refused to believe me.
I went on to ask what he thought of doing as a preliminary,
to earn some little reputation in another direction, which perchance might be of assistance to the execution of his soaring
plan.

This seemed to dispel his ill-humour. 'Listen!' he answered:
'You know that I have always had a strong preference for
instrumental music. Here in Paris, where a regular cult of our
great Beethoven appears to have been instituted, I have reason
to hope that his fellow-countryman and most ardent worshipper
will easily find admittance when he undertakes to give the public
a hearing of his own attempts, however feeble, to follow in the
footsteps of that great master.'

'Excuse me for cutting you short,' I interposed. 'Beethoven
indeed is becoming deified; in that you are right. But, mind you,
it is his name, his renown that is deified. That name, prefixed
to a work not unworthy of the great master, will suffice to secure

its beauties instant recognition. By any other name, however, the selfsame work will never gain the attention of the directorate of a concert management, however brilliant it may be.'

'You lie!' my friend exclaimed hastily. 'Your purpose is becoming clear, to systematically discourage me, and frighten me from the path of fame. You shall not succeed, however!'

'I know you,' I replied, 'and forgive you. Nevertheless I must point out that you will stumble on the very same difficulties which confront every artist without a name, however great his talent, in a place where people have far too little time to bother themselves about hidden treasures. Your plans are methods of fortifying an already established position, and gaining profit from it, but they are by no means likely to win you such a position. People will either pay no heed at all to your application for a performance of your instrumental compositions, or, if your works are composed in that daring individual spirit which you so much admire in Beethoven, they will find them turgid and indigestible, and send you home with a flea in your ear.'

'But,' my friend put in, 'what if I have already circumvented such a reproach? What if I have written works expressly to commend me to a more superficial public, and have adorned them with those favourite modern effects which I abhor from the bottom of my heart, but which are not despised by even considerable artists as preliminary bids for favour?'

'They will give you to understand,' I replied, 'that your work is too light, too shallow, to be brought to the public ear between the creations of a Beethoven and a Musard.'

'Dear man!' my friend exclaimed. 'That's good indeed! At last I see that you are making fun of me. You always were a wag!' My friend stamped his foot and laughed, and trod so forcibly upon the lordly paw of his splendid dog that the latter yelped aloud, then licked his master's hand, and seemed humbly to beg him not to take any more of my objections as jokes.

'You see,' I said, 'it is not always well to take earnestness as jest. But never mind, tell me what other plans could have moved you to exchange your modest home for this dreadful Paris. In what other way, if you will provisionally abandon the two plans you have spoken of, do you propose to make a name for yourself?'

'So be it,' was the reply I received. 'In spite of your singular love of contradiction, I will proceed with the narration of my plans. Nothing, as I know, is more popular in Paris drawing-rooms than those charming sentimental ballads and romances, which are so much enjoyed by the French, and some of which have even been imported from our fatherland. Think of Franz Schubert's songs, and the vogue they enjoy here! This is a genre that admirably suits my inclination; I feel capable of turning out something worth noticing there. I will get my songs sung, and perhaps I may share the good luck which has fallen to so many, namely of attracting by these unpretentious works the attention of some Director of the Opéra who may happen to be present, so that he honours me with the commission for an opera.'

The dog again uttered a violent howl. This time it was I who, in an agony of laughter, had trodden on the paw of the excellent beast.

'What?' I cried. 'Is it possible that you seriously entertain such an idiotic idea? What on earth could have encouraged you – '

'My God!' the enthusiast broke in, 'have not similar instances happened often enough? Must I bring you the newspapers in which I have repeatedly read how such-and-such a Director was so carried away by the hearing of a romance, how such-and-such a famous poet was suddenly so impressed by the talent of a totally unknown composer, that both of them at once united in the resolve, the one to supply him with a libretto, the other to produce the opera to be written to order?'

'Ah! is that it?' I sighed, filled with sudden sadness. 'Press notices have led your simple childlike head astray. Dear friend, don't believe more than a third of what you read, and don't even trust all of that! Our Directors have better things to do, than to hear romances sung over which they fall into raptures.

D

And, even if that were a feasible mode of gaining a reputation, by whom would you get your romances sung?'

'By whom else,' was the rejoinder, 'than the same world-famous singers who have so often, and with such great amiability, made it their duty to introduce the productions of unknown or neglected talent to the public? Or am I here again deceived by lying paragraphs?'

'My friend,' I replied, 'God knows how little I wish to deny that noble hearts of this kind beat below the throats of our foremost singers, male and female. But to attain the honour of such patronage, one needs at least some other essentials. You can easily imagine what competition goes on here also, and that it requires an infinitely influential recommendation, to make it dawn upon those noble hearts that one really is an unknown genius. Poor friend, have you no other plans?'

Here my companion took leave of his senses. In a violent passion, though with some regard for his dog, he turned away from me. 'If I had as many more plans as the sands of the sea,' he shouted, 'you should not hear a single one of them. Go! You are my enemy! Yet know, inexorable man, you shall not triumph over me! Tell me, the last question I will put to you, tell me, wretch, how then have the myriads commenced, who first became known, and finally famous, in Paris?'

'Ask one of them,' I replied, with somewhat ruffled composure, 'and perhaps you may discover. For my part, I don't know.'

'Here, here!' called the infatuated man to his wonderful dog. 'You are my friend no longer,' he volleyed at me. 'Your cold derision shall not make me blench. In one year from now – remember this – in one year from now, either every street-urchin will be able to tell you where I live, or you shall hear from me whither to come to see me die. Farewell!'

He whistled shrilly and discordantly to his dog. He and his superb companion vanished like a flash of lightning. I had no chance of overtaking them.

It was only after a few days, when all my efforts to ascertain where my friend was lodging had proved futile, that I began to realise the wrong I had done in not showing more consideration for the peculiarities of so profoundly enthusiastic a nature, and with my brusque, perhaps exaggerated, objections to his very innocent plans. With the worthy intention of dissuading him from his projects as much as possible, because I did not deem him fitted either by his outward or his inward condition successfully to pursue so intricate a path to fame, I had not reckoned with the fact that I was not dealing with one of those tractable and easily persuaded natures, but with a man whose deep belief in the divine and irrefutable genius of his art had reached such a pitch of fanaticism, that it had turned one of the gentlest of tempers to a dogged obstinacy.

Most probably, I thought, he is now wandering through the streets of Paris in the firm conviction that he has only to decide which of his plans to realise first, in order to figure at once on one of those poster-advertisements that inform us of forthcoming musical performances. He may even be giving an old beggar a sou today, with the determination to make it a golden napoleon a few months hence.

As more and more time slipped by after our initial encounter, and the more fruitless my endeavours to unearth my friend became, I must admit I began to be infected by the confidence he had displayed. I allowed myself to search the advertisements of musical performances, now and again, straining my eyes to discover in some corner of them the name of my confident enthusiast. And the less success I had in these attempts at discovery, the greater, remarkable to say, became my friendly interest allied with an ever-increasing belief that my friend might perhaps succeed; that perchance even now, while I was seeking anxiously for him, his peculiar talent might already have been discovered and acknowledged by some important person or other; that perhaps he had received one of those commissions whose happy execution brings fortune, honour, and God knows what else. And why not? Is there not a star to guide the destiny of every inspired soul? Might not his be a lucky star? Cannot miracles occur, and hidden treasure be discovered? The very fact that I saw no announcement of a single romance, overture or the like, under the name of my friend, made me believe that he had gone straight for his most grandiose plan and, despising those lesser aids to publicity, was already up to his eyes at work on an opera of at least five acts. True, I had never come across him in the haunts of artists, or met anyone at all who knew anything about him. Still, as my own attendance at those sanctuaries was but rare, it was conceivable that it was I who was the unfortunate one, who could not penetrate where his friend's fame perhaps already shone with dazzling rays.

You may easily guess that it took a considerable time for my first sad interest in my friend to change into a confident belief in his good star. It was only through all the phases of fear, of doubt, of hope, that I could arrive at this point. Such things are somewhat slow with me, and so it happened that almost a year had already elapsed since the day when I met that splendid dog and my enthusiastic friend in the Palais-Royal. Meanwhile some wonderfully lucky speculations had brought me to so unprecedented a pitch of prosperity that, like Polycrates of old, I began to fear an imminent reverse. I fancied I could plainly see it coming. Thus it was in a gloomy frame of mind, that one day I took my customary walk in the Champs-Elysées.

It was autumn. The leaves fell withered from the trees, and the sky hung grey with age above the Elysian pomp below. But, nothing daunted, the Punch and Judy show was presented daily. Punch renewed his perennial mad onslaught. In a blind rage the scoundrel constantly defied the justice of this world, until at last the daemonic principle, so forcibly depicted by the chained-up cat with superhuman claws, laid low the saucy ebullience of the presumptuous mortal.

Close by my side, a few yards from the humble scene of Punch's misdeeds I heard the following remarkable soliloquy in German: 'Excellent! excellent! Why, in the name of all the world, have I allowed myself to seek so far, when I could have

found so near? What? Am I to despise this stage, on which the
most thrilling political and poetic truths are set in realistic guise,
so directly and intelligibly, before the most receptive and least
assuming public? Is this braggart not Don Giovanni? Is that
astonishingly white cat not the Commendatore on horseback, in
very person? How the artistic import of this drama will be
heightened and transfigured when my music adds its quota!
What sonorous organs in these actors! And the cat – ah, that
cat! What hidden charms lie buried in her glorious throat!
Now she gives no sound, now she is nothing but a demon: but
how fascinating she will be when she sings the roulades I shall
write expressly for her! What a magnificent *portamento* she'll
put into the execution of that supernatural chromatic scale!
How treacherous will be her smile, when she sings that famous
passage of the future: '*O Punch, thou art lost!*' What an idea!
And then, what a splendid pretext for incessant use of the big
drum Punch's constant truncheon-beats afford me! Come, why
delay? Quick, I'll seek the Director's favour! Here I can walk
straight in, no antechambers here! With one step I'm in the
sanctuary, before him whose godlike piercing eye will recognise
at once my genius. Or shall I encounter competition here as well?
Should the cat – ? Quick, before it is too late!'

With these last words the soliloquist was about to make
straight for the Punch and Judy box. I had speedily recognised
my friend, and, determined to avert a scandal, I seized him
by the arm, and turned him round towards me.

'Who is it?' he cried irritably. He soon recognised me, quietly
detached himself, and added coldly: 'I might have known
that it could only be *you* who would thwart me in this as well,
my last hope of salvation. Leave me. It may soon be too late.'

I grasped him again, but, although I was able to stop him
from rushing forward to the little theatre, it was quite impossible
to move him from the spot. Still, I gained the leisure to observe
him closely. Great heavens, what a condition he was in. I say
nothing of his clothes, but of his features. The former were poor
and threadbare, but the latter were terrible. The free and open

look was gone. Lifeless and vacant, his eye travelled to and fro; his pallid, sunken cheeks spoke of worse than mere trouble. The hectic flush upon them told of sufferings too, and of hunger!

As I studied him in great sorrow, he too seemed touched, for he struggled less to tear himself away from me.

'How goes it with you, dear Robert?' I asked, my voice choking. With a mournful smile I added: 'Where is your beautiful dog?'

He looked black at once. 'Stolen!' was the abrupt reply.

'Not sold?' I asked again.

'Wretch,' he sullenly replied, 'are you also like the Englishman?'

I did not understand his meaning. 'Come,' I said in faltering tones. 'Come! take me to your house. I have much to speak to you about.'

'You will soon know my house without my aid,' he answered. 'The year is not yet up. I'm now on the high road to recognition, fortune! Go, you do not yet believe it! What use is it to preach to the deaf? You people must *see*, to believe. Very well! You shall soon see. But let go of me now, or I shall consider you my sworn enemy.'

I gripped his hands more tightly. 'Where do you live?' I asked. 'Come, take me there! We'll have a friendly, hearty chat about your plans, if it must be so!'

'You shall learn them as soon as they are carried out,' he answered. 'Quadrilles, galops! Oh, that is my forte! You shall see and hear! Do you see that cat? She's to help me get huge fees! See how sleek she is, how daintily she licks her chops! Imagine the effect when from that little mouth, between those pearly rows of teeth, the most inspired of chromatic scales bursts forth, accompanied by the most delicate moans and sobs in all the world! Imagine it, dear friend! Oh, you have no sense of fantasy, you! Leave me, leave me! You have no imagination.'

I held him tighter, and implored him to conduct me to his lodgings. I was making no effect on him at all, however. His eye was fixed anxiously upon the cat.

'Everything depends on her,' he cried. 'Fortune, honour, fame, reside within her velvet paws. May Heaven guide her heart, and turn on me her favour! She looks friendly, yes, that's the feline nature! And she *is* friendly, polite, polite beyond measure! But she's a cat, a false and treacherous cat! Wait, I know how to subdue you. I have a noble dog. He'll make you respect me. Victory! I've won the day! Where is my dog?'

He had shot forth the last few words in mad excitement, with a piercing cry. He looked hastily round, as if seeking for his dog. His eager glance fell on the roadway. There rode past upon a splendid horse an elegant gentleman, who judging by his physiognomy and the peculiar cut of his clothes was an Englishman. By his side ran, proudly barking, my friend's fine Newfoundland dog.

'Ha! My presentiment!' shrieked my friend, in a fury of wrath at the sight. 'The cursed brute! My dog! my dog!' My strength was unavailing against the violence with which the unhappy creature tore himself away. Like an arrow he fled after the horseman, who happened just then to be spurring his horse to a gallop, which the dog accompanied with the liveliest gambols. I rushed after, but in vain! What strength can compare with the feats of a madman? I saw the rider, the dog, my friend, all vanish down one of the side streets that lead to the Faubourg du Roule. When I reached the same street, they were gone.

I need hardly mention that all my endeavours to track them were fruitless. Alarmed, and almost driven to madness myself, I was forced at last to give up my inquiries for the moment. But you may readily imagine that I none the less bestirred myself each day to find some clue to the hiding-place of my unhappy friend. I sought for news in every place that had the remotest connection with music: nowhere was there the smallest sign! It was only in the sacred antechambers of the Opéra that the meanest officials remembered a pitiable apparition, which had often presented itself and waited for an audience, but of whose name or dwelling they were naturally ignorant. Every other path, even the police, led to no further traces. The guardians of public safety seemed to think it unnecessary to concern themselves about the poor soul.

I fell into despair. Then one day, about two months after that affair in the Champs-Elysées, I received a letter forwarded to me in a roundabout fashion through one of my acquaintances. I opened it with a heavy heart, and read the brief words: *'Dear friend, come and see me die!'*

The address denoted a narrow little street in Montmartre. It was no time for tears, and I ascended the hill of Montmartre. Following the directions, I arrived at one of those poverty-stricken houses which are common enough in the side-alleys of that little district. Despite its poor exterior, this building boasted five storeys. My unfortunate friend would appear to have welcomed the fact, and thus I, too, was compelled to mount to the same giddy height. It was worth while, for, on asking for my friend, I was referred to the back attic. From this hinder side of the estimable building one certainly had no view of the four-foot-wide magnificence of the street, but one was rewarded by the incomparably finer view of the whole of Paris.

I found my poor enthusiast propped up on a wretched sick-bed, drinking in this wonderful prospect. His face, his whole body, were infinitely more haggard and emaciated than on that day in the Champs-Elysées; nevertheless the expression of his features was far more reassuring. The scared, wild, almost maniacal look, the uncanny fire in his eyes, had vanished. His glance was dulled and half extinguished; the dark and ghastly flecks upon his cheeks seemed quenched in a universal wasting.

Trembling, but still composed, he stretched his hand out to me with the words: 'Forgive me, old fellow, and receive my thanks for coming.'

The softness and sonority of the tone in which he uttered these few words produced on me an even more touching impression, if possible, than his appearance had already done. I pressed his hand, but could not speak for weeping.

'I think,' went on my friend, after an affecting pause, 'it is already well over a year, since we met in that glittering Palais-

Royal. I have not quite kept my word: to become renowned within a year, was impossible for me, with the best will in the world. On the other hand, it's no fault of mine that I could not write to you punctually upon the year's end, to tell you where to come to see me die. Despite all my struggles, I had not yet got quite so far. No, do not weep, my friend! There was a time when I had to beg you not to laugh.'

I tried to speak, but speech forsook me. 'Let me speak!' the dying man put in. 'It is becoming easy to me, and I owe you a long account. I'm sure that I shall not be here tomorrow, so listen to my narrative today! It's a simple tale, my friend, most simple. In it you'll find no wondrous complications, no hairbreadth strokes of luck, no ostentatious details. Do not worry that your patience will be exhausted by the ease of speech which now is granted to me, and which certainly might tempt me to long-windedness; for there have been days, dear old man, when I couldn't utter a sound. Listen! When I reflect on the state in which you find me, I consider it needless to inform you that my fate has been no bright one. Nor do I need to recount to you the trivialities among which my enthusiasm has been wrecked. Suffice it to say, that they were not rocks, on which I foundered! Happy the shipwrecked soul who goes down in a storm! No, they were quagmires and swamps, in which I sank. These swamps, dear friend, surround all proud and dazzling fountains of art, to which we poor fools make such ardent pilgrimage, as though they held the salvation of our souls. The feather-brained man is happier! With one successful *entrechat* he leaps the quagmire. The rich man is happier! His well-trained horse needs but one prick of the golden spur, to bear him swiftly across. But woe to the enthusiast who, taking that swamp for a flowery meadow, is swallowed in it past all recourse, a meal for frogs and toads! See, dear friend, this vermin has devoured me. There's not a drop of blood left in me! Must I tell you how it happened? But why? You see I am done for. Be content to hear that I was not vanquished on the field of battle, but that – horrible to utter – I fell in the antechambers of hunger. They are something terrible, those antechambers. I must tell you that there are many, very many of them in Paris, with seats of wood or velvet, heated and not heated, paved and unpaved!

'In those antechambers,' continued my friend, 'I dreamed away a fair year of my life. I dreamed of many wondrous mad and fabled stories from the *Arabian Nights*, of men and beasts, of gold and offal. My dreams were of gods and bassoon players, of jewelled snuff-boxes and prima donnas, of satin gowns and lovesick lords, of chorus-girls and five-franc pieces. Between whiles I sometimes seemed to hear the wailing, ghost-like note of an oboe. That note thrilled through my every nerve, and pierced my heart. One day when I had dreamed my maddest, and that oboe-note was tingling through me at its sharpest, I suddenly awoke and found I had become a madman. At least I recollected that I had forgotten to make my usual obeisance to the theatre-lackey as I left the ante-room; the reason, I may add, why I never dared to return to it, for how would the man have received me? With tottering steps I left the haven of my dreams. On the threshold of the building I fell in a heap. I had stumbled over my poor dog, who, after his wont, was ante-chambering in the street, waiting for his fortunate master who was allowed to antechamber among men. This dog, I must tell you, had been of the utmost service to me, for to him and his beauty alone I owed the fact that now and then the lackey of the antechamber would honour me with a passing glance. Alas, with every day that passed he lost a portion of his beauty, for hunger gnawed his entrails too. This gave me further alarm, as I clearly foresaw that the servant's favour would soon be lost to me. Already a contemptuous smile would often hover round his lips. As I said, I fell over this dog of mine. How long I lay there, I do not know. Of the kicks which I may have received from passers-by I took no notice; but at last I was awoken by the tenderest of kisses, by the warm licks of my dear beast. I leapt to my feet, and in a lucid interval I recognised at once where my duty lay. I must buy the dog some food. A shrewd old-clothes dealer gave me a handful of sous for my villainous waistcoat. My dog ate, and what he left I devoured. This suited him admirably, but I was past mending. The proceeds from an heirloom, an old ring of my grandmother's, sufficed to restore the dog to his former beauty; he bloomed anew. Oh, fatal blooming!

'My brain became increasingly disordered. I do not know what took place within it, but I remember being seized one day by an irresistible longing to seek out the Devil. My dog, in all his former glory, accompanied me to the gates of the Concerts Musard. Did I hope to meet the Devil there? That also I cannot tell. I scanned the people trooping in, and whom did I espy among them? The abominable Englishman. The same man, as large as life, and not one atom changed from when, as I related to you, he harmed me so with Beethoven! I was seized with fear; I was prepared to face a demon from the nether world, but not this phantom of the upper. What I suffered when the wretch also recognised *me*! I couldn't avoid him, the crowd was pressing us towards each other. Involuntarily, and quite against the custom of his countrymen, he was compelled to fall into my arms, which I had raised up to force an exit for myself. There he lay, wedged tight against my breast, with its thousand torturing emotions. It was a fearful moment! We were soon able to release ourselves a little, and he shook me off with a shade of indignation. I tried then to escape, but it was impossible. "Welcome, mein Herr!" the Englishman shouted. "I always meet you on the paths of art! This time we'll go to the concert together!"

'For very wrath I could say nothing but: "To the Devil!"

' "Quite so," he answered, "it seems that things go devilish well in there! Last Sunday I threw off a composition, which I shall offer to Musard. Do you know this Musard? Will you introduce me to him?"

'My horror at this bugbear turned to speechless fear, which gave me the strength to free myself and flee towards the boulevard. My lovely dog rushed barking after me. But in a trice the Englishman was by my side once more, holding me, and asking in excited tones: "Sir, does this splendid dog belong to you?"

' "Yes."

' "But it is superb! I will pay you fifty guineas for this dog, sir. A dog like this, you know, is the proper thing for a gentleman, and I have already owned a number of them. Unfortunately, the beasts were all unmusical; they could not stand my practising the horn or flute, and so they always ran away. But I take it for granted that, as you have the good fortune to be a musician, your dog is also musical. I may therefore hope that he will stay with me. So I offer you fifty guineas for the beast."

' "Villain!" I cried, "not for the whole of Britain would I sell my friend!" So saying, I hurried off, my dog in front of me. I dodged down the back streets that led to my usual lodging. It was bright moonshine. Now and then I looked furtively back : to my alarm, I thought I saw the Englishman's tall figure following me. I redoubled my speed, and peered round still more anxiously. Now I caught sight of the shadow, now lost it. Panting for breath, I reached my refuge, gave my dog some food, and threw myself hungry on my rough, hard bed. I slept long, and dreamed of horrors. When I awoke, my beautiful dog had vanished. How he had got away from me, or been enticed through the ill-fastened door, to this day is a mystery to me. I called, I hunted for him, until, sobbing, I fainted away.

'You remember that I saw the faithless creature again one day in the Champs-Elysées. You know what efforts I made to regain possession of him, but what you do not know is that this animal recognised me, yet fled from my call like an untamed wild beast! Nevertheless I followed him and his Satanic cavalier until the latter dashed into a gateway, whose doors were slammed behind him and the dog. In my anger I thundered at the gates. A furious bark was the answer. Dazed and crushed, I leant against the archway, until at last a hideous scale played on the horn aroused me from my stupefaction; it reached me from the ground floor of the mansion, and was followed by the agonised moan of a dog. Then I laughed out loud, and went on my way.'

My friend ceased speaking. Though speech had become easy, his inward agitation taxed him terribly. It was no longer possible for him to hold himself erect in bed. With a smothered groan he sank back. A long pause followed. I watched the poor fellow with painful feelings: that faint flush so peculiar to the consumptive had risen to his cheeks. He had closed his eyes, and lay as if in slumber. His breath came lightly, almost in ethereal waves.

I waited anxiously for the moment when I might dare to speak to him, and ask what earthly service I could render. At last he opened his eyes once more. A dim but wondrous light was in the glance he straightway fixed on me.

'My poor friend,' I began, 'I came here with the sad desire to serve you somehow. Have you any wish? Tell me!'

With a smile he resumed: 'Are you so impatient, my friend, for my last testament? No, have no care. You too are mentioned in it. But will you not first learn how it befell that your poor brother came to die? Listen, I wanted my history to be known to one soul at least; but I know of no one who would worry himself about me, except yourself. Do not fear that I am overexerting myself! All is well with me and easy, no laboured breath oppresses me, the words come freely to my lips. And see, I have little left to narrate. You can imagine that, from the point where I broke off my story, I had no more outside events to deal with. From there begins the history of my inner life, for then I knew I would soon quit this earth. That terrible scale on the horn in the Englishman's hotel filled me with so overpowering a weariness of life, that I there and then resolved to die. Indeed, I should not boast of that decision, for I must confess that it no longer lay entirely within my own free will. Something had cracked within my breast, something that left a long and whirring sound behind. When this died down, all was light and well with me, as never before, and I knew my end was near. Oh how happy that knowledge made me! How the presentiment of a speedy dissolution cheered me, as I suddenly perceived its effect on every member of this wasted body. Insensible to outward things, unconscious where my faltering steps were bearing me, I had gained the summit of Montmartre. Thrice welcoming the

Mount of Martyrs, I resolved to die on it. I too was dying for the wholeness of my faith. I too could therefore call myself a martyr, although my faith was challenged only by hunger.

'Homeless, I took this lodging, asking for nothing more than this bed, and that they would send for my scores and papers, which I had stowed in a wretched hovel in the city, for, alas, I had never succeeded in pawning them. So here I lie, determined to pass away in thoughts of God and pure music. A friend will close my eyes, my effects will cover all my debts, and, I shall not lack a decent grave. Tell me, what more could I wish?'

At last I gave vent to my pent-up feelings. 'What!' I cried, 'was it only for this last mournful service, that you could use me? Could your friend, however powerless, have helped you in nothing else? I beg you, for my own peace of mind tell me this: was it because you doubted my friendship, that you didn't discover my whereabouts sooner and acquaint me with your distress?'

'Oh, don't be angry,' he answered coaxingly. 'Don't chide me if I confess that I had fallen into the stubborn belief that you were my enemy! When I recognised that you were not, my brain was already in a condition that robbed me of all willpower. I felt that I was no longer fit to associate with men of sense. Forgive me, and be kinder towards me than I have been to you! Give me your hand, and let this debt of my poor life be cancelled!'

I could not resist, but seized his hand, and melted into tears. Yet I saw how fast the powers of my friend were ebbing. He was now too weak to raise himself in bed. His sunken cheeks were noticeably paler.

'A little business, dear friend,' he began afresh. 'Call it my last will and testament! For I wish, in the first place, that my debts should be paid. The poor people who took me in have nursed me willingly and charged me little. They must be paid. The same with a few other creditors, whose names you will find on that paper. I bequeath all my property in payment; there are my compositions and here is my diary, in which I have jotted down my musical whims and reflections. I leave it to your judgment, my experienced friend, to sell as much of these remains as will liquidate my earthly debts. My second request is that you do not beat my dog, if you should ever meet him. I assume that, in punishment of his faithlessness, he has already suffered torments from the Englishman's horn. I forgive him! Thirdly, I wish the history of my Paris sufferings, with the omission of my name, to be published as a wholesome warning to all soft fools like me. Fourthly, I wish for a decent grave, yet without any fuss or ceremony. There are very few people to be invited, and their names and addresses you'll find in my diary. The costs of the burial must be mustered up by you and them. Amen!

'Now,' the dying man continued, after a pause occasioned by his growing weakness, 'now one last word on my belief. I believe in God, Mozart and Beethoven, and likewise their disciples and apostles. I believe in the Holy Spirit and the truth of the one, indivisible Art. I believe that this Art proceeds from God, and lives within the hearts of all artists. I believe that he who once has bathed in the sublime delights of this high Art, is consecrated to Her for ever, and never can deny Her. I believe that through this Art all men are saved, and therefore each may die of hunger for Her. I believe that death will give me my highest happiness. I believe that on earth I was a jarring discord, which will at once be perfectly resolved by death. I believe in a last judgment, which will condemn to fearful pains all those who in this world have dared to play the huckster with chaste Art, have violated and dishonoured Her through the evilness of their hearts and the ribald lust of their senses. I believe that these will be condemned through all eternity to hear their own vile music. I believe, upon the other hand, that true disciples of high Art will be transfigured in a heavenly veil of sun-drenched fragrance of sweet sound, and united for eternity with the divine fount of all Harmony. May mine be a sentence of grace! Amen!'

I could almost believe that my friend's fervent prayer had been granted already, so heavenly was the light that shone in his eye, so enraptured did he remain in breathless quiet. But his gentle, scarcely palpable breathing assured me that he yet lived on. Softly, but quite audibly, he whispered : 'Rejoice, ye faithful ones; the joy is great, towards which ye journey!'

Then he grew dumb, the radiance of his glance was quenched. A smile still wreathed his lips. I closed his eyes, and prayed God for such a death.

Who knows what died in this child of man, leaving no trace behind? Was it a Mozart, a Beethoven? Who can tell, and who gainsay me when I claim that in him there fell an artist who would have enriched the world with his creations, had he not been forced to die too soon of hunger. I repeat, who will prove the contrary? None of those who followed his body. Besides myself there were but two, a philologist and a painter. A third was hindered by a cold, and the others had no time to spare. As we were quietly approaching the churchyard of Montmartre, we noticed a beautiful dog, who anxiously sniffed at the bier and coffin. I recognised the animal, and looked behind me. Sitting bolt upright on his horse was the Englishman. He seemed unable to understand the strange behaviour of his dog, who followed the coffin into the graveyard. He dismounted, gave the reins to his groom, and overtook us in the cemetery.

'Whom are you burying, mein Herr?' he asked me. 'The master of that dog,' I replied.

'Goddam it!' he cried. 'It is most annoying that this gentleman should have died without receiving the money for his beast. I set it aside for him, and have sought an opportunity of sending it, although this animal howls at my musical exercises like all the rest. But I will make good my omission, and devote the fifty guineas for the dog to a memorial stone, which shall be erected on the grave of the estimable gentleman!' He left us, and mounted his horse. The dog remained beside the grave, and the Englishman rode away.

On Opera Libretti and Combosition

Über das Opern-Dichten und Komponieren im Besonderen first appeared in the *Bayreuther Blätter* in September 1879, and was reprinted in Volume 10 of the collected works.

*

I have been struck on various occasions by how little the audience at opera performances is acquainted with the matter of the plot. Great classical operas such as *Don Giovanni* and *Figaro* may benefit from this when there are innocent youthful hearers, especially of the female sex. They have no knowledge of the frivolities in the text – a lack which guardians and teachers may well have counted on when they expressly commended these works to their pupils as models of pure taste. The fact that the happenings in *Robert the Devil* and *The Huguenots*[1] may be intelligible to none but the inmost circle of initiates, has much in its favour; but that *Der Freischütz* too should remain obscure, as I lately discovered, amazed me, until a little thought convinced me that, although I had conducted this opera any number of times in the orchestra, I myself was still quite hazy as to many passages in the text. Some people lay the blame on our singers' indistinctness of delivery. When I objected that, in dialogue operas such as *Freischütz*, *Zauberflöte*, and our German translations of *Don Giovanni* and *Figaro*, everything that explains the action is actually spoken, I was reminded that the singers of

[1] By Meyerbeer.

our day *speak* indistinctly too, and also that, for this very
reason perhaps, the dialogue is abridged to unintelligibility.
This makes matters worse; for, with operas composed throughout
(i.e. with no intervening recitative), one can at least arrive at
sufficient understanding of the scenic action with the help of the
textbook, whereas, in books which contain the words only of the
arias of dialogue operas, such an aid is not forthcoming. I have
noticed that, for the most part, German audiences learn nothing
at all of what the poet really meant with his libretto. Often
enough, even the composer appears not to know. With the
French it is different. Their first question is as to the overall
piece. The play must be entertaining in and for itself, except
perhaps in the case of the lofty genre of 'Grand Opera', where
ballet has to provide the fun. The texts of Italian operas, on the
other hand, are fairly trivial as a rule, the virtuosity of the
singers appearing to be the main concern; yet the Italian singer
cannot rise to the level of his task without a remarkably clear
enunciation, quite indispensable to his vocal phrasing, and we
do the Italian operatic genre a great injustice when we slur the
texts of arias in our German performances. Mechanical as is the
Italian type of operatic composition, I still find that it has a
better effect when the text is understood than when it is not,
since a knowledge of the situation and exact emotion will help
to ward off the effect of monotony in the musical expression.
Only in the case of Rossini's *Semiramide* did I find that even this
knowledge was of no help to me. Reissiger's[2] *Dido abbandonata*,
which earned its composer the favour of a Saxon monarch, I do
not know, any more than F. Hiller's[3] *Romilda*.

If the above observations are correct, one could simply attribute the German public's love of opera performances to its
pleasure in hearing the separate numbers, as purely melodic
entities *per se*. The Italians long ago attained great skill in
manufacturing such pieces, so that it was only recently that the
German composer dared to vie with them. When Mozart had

[2] Karl Reissiger (1798-1859).
[3] Ferdinand Hiller (1811-1885).

to compose *Die Zauberflöte* he was worried as to whether he
would do it successfully, as he 'had composed no magic operas
before'. With what aplomb, on the contrary, he treated *Le
nozze di Figaro* : on the foundation of Italian *opera buffa*
he reared a building of such perfect symmetry that he was
easily able to decline to sacrifice a single note to his Emperor
who demanded cuts.[4] What the Italians threw in as banal links
and interludes between the numbers proper, Mozart used vigor-
ously to animate the plot, in striking harmony with the exception-
ally finished comedy text that lay before him. Just as in the
symphonies of Beethoven the very pauses grow eloquent, so here
the noisy half-closes and cadences which might well have added
little to the Mozartian symphony give a quite irreplaceable life
to the scenic action, where craft and presence of mind fight,
lovelessly, with passion and brutality. Here the dialogue becomes
all music, whilst the music converses; a thing that certainly
was only possible because the master developed the orchestra
to a pitch that had never before been dreamt of, and which has
perhaps not been attempted since. On the other hand, pieces
which had been isolated before became fused into what appeared
to be so complete a piece of music that the admirable comedy
on which it was based was finally altogether overlooked, and
nothing heard but music. So it seemed to our musicians; and
Mozart's *Figaro* was given more carelessly and indistinctly day
by day, until at last we have arrived at the point where we
perform this work in such a way that our teachers have no
scruples in sending their pupils to the theatre on *Figaro* nights.

We will not discuss any further the effect of these instances of
public vandalism on the German's sensibility to the genuine
and correct; but it is important to note their misleading influence on the drafts and finished products of our own operatic
poets and composers. Forsaking their native terrain, they sought
at first to emulate the ready-made Italian opera. This led to the

---

4 When Joseph I told Mozart he thought *Die Entführung aus dem Serail*
contained a great many notes, the composer is reputed to have replied,
'Not one too many, Sire.'

closest possible imitation of the Italian cabaletta, and the aban-
donment of every broader mode of musical conception. No
emphasis was laid upon the rhyme and reason of the whole.
Did it really matter if in *Die Zauberflöte*, composed for a German
text and spoken with German dialogue, the villain was suddenly
changed to a hero, the originally good woman to a bad one,
making utter nonsense of what had happened in the first act?
Nevertheless it was difficult for the German genius to master
the Italian cabaletta. Even Weber in his very young days tried in
vain to make something of the coloratura aria, and it needed the
heart-stirring years of the War of Liberation to set this composer,
the musician of Korner's poems, on his own feet. *Der Freischütz*
has given us in Germany something that few nations have been
fortunate enough to have.

But we are not attempting here to trace the historic evolution
of German opera, we are merely explaining the peculiar difficulties attendant on that evolution by referring to German opera's
fundamental faults. The chief of these I find is the criminal
vagueness that has disfigured all our opera performances from
the very beginning, as I stated in my prefatory words. I have
touched on the cause of this, the librettist's and composer's lack
of concern with the literary standards of the libretto, in the
previous paragraphs. The so-called *tragédie lyrique,* which
reached Germany from abroad, remained of no consequence and
unintelligible to us unless the aria took the composer's fancy by
its marked melodic structure. This aria form of melody remained
the sole aim and end of the composer of German operas, and
thus of the poet also. The latter felt that he might relax somewhat
in the text for an aria, as the composer had his own musical
scheme for extension, interchange and repetition of themes, and
the poet had an entirely free hand with the words, which he
would repeat at pleasure either as a whole or in part. Long lines
could only hamper the composer, whilst a stanza of about four
lines was ample measure for one section of an aria. The verbal
repetitions necessary to fill out the melody, conceived quite apart
from the verse, even gave the composer opportunity for pleasant

variations on the so-called declamation through a shifting of accents. In Winter's *Opferfest* we find this rule observed throughout. In it, one of the characters sings 'Mein *Leben* hab' ich ihm zu danken' ('I owe him my *life*'), and then immediately afterwards, 'Mein Leben *hab*' ich ihm zu danken' ('I *owe* him my life'). He goes on to repeat a question in the form of an answer:

> Muss nicht der Mensch auch menschlich sein?
> Der Mensch muss menschlich sein.

> Should not man also be humane?
> Man must be humane.

Marschner once had the grave misfortune, in his *Adolf von Nassau*, to triplicate the words 'hat sie' ('has she') on a particularly incisive rhythmic accent:

Even Weber could not avoid the temptation to vary the accent. His Euryanthe sings: 'Was ist mein Leben gegen *diesen* Augenblick,' ('What is my life compared to *this* moment'), and repeats it as: 'Was ist mein Leben gegen diesen *Auge*nblick' ('What is my life compared to this *mom*ent')! This sort of thing leads the hearer away from any serious attention to the words, without affording adequate compensation in the purely musical phrase itself, for in most cases it is merely a question of musico-rhetorical flourishes, such as are seen at their most naïve in Rossini's eternal 'Felicitàs'.

It seems, however, that it was not solely the delight in a free use of flourishes that prompted the composer to his arbitrary dealings with parts of the text. No, the whole relationship of verse to the truthfulness of musical accent gave the composer from the beginning the choice of either declaiming the text in strict accordance with the accent of daily speech and common sense, which would have resolved the verse with all its rhymes into naked prose; or, regardless of that accent, completely subjecting the words to certain dance-rhythms, and giving free rein to melodic invention. The results of this latter method were far less destructive, or even disturbing, with the Italians and French than with ourselves, because their speaking-accent is incomparably more accommodating and, in particular, not bound to the root-syllable; and also, they do not weigh the feet in their metres, but simply count them. Through our bad translations of their texts, however, we had acquired from them that peculiar operatic jargon in which we thought it fit, and even requisite, to declaim our own German lines. Certainly, the more conscientious composers were finally disgusted with this frivolous maltreatment of our tongue : but it still never occurred to them that even the verse of our first-class poets was not real, melody-invoking verse, but merely elaborate sham. Weber declared it his duty to reproduce the text faithfully, yet admitted that, were he always to do so, he would have to say goodbye to his melody. In fact it was exactly this striving of Weber's to preserve the set divisions of the verse-text and thereby make the thought intelligible, which, coupled with his adherence to a melodic pattern for the resulting incongruities, led to that indistinctness whereof I promised to quote an example. This occurs in Max's aria in *Der Freischütz* : 'Durch die Wälder, durch die Auen'. Here the poet had committed the egregious blunder of furnishing the composer with the following verse :

> Abends bracht' ich reiche Beute,
> Und wie über eig'nes Glück –
> Drohend wohl dem Mörder – freute
> Sich Agathens Liebesblick.

In the evenings I brought back a rich bag,
And as though over her own good fortune –
Dangerous though it was for the slayer –
Agathe's loving glance rejoiced.

Now, Weber really takes the trouble to phrase these lines in strict accordance with their sense and sequence: he therefore makes a break after the parenthesis 'drohend wohl dem Mörder', and begins the closing musical line with 'freute'; but as that makes the line much longer, he feels obliged to employ the verb – so important for a connection with the second line – as a preliminary 'arsis'; whereas the pronoun 'sich', merely introduced to supplement the verb, receives the stronger accent of the following beat. Admittedly, this has resulted in an entrancing strain of melody:

"Abends bracht' ich rei-che Beute, und wie ü - ber eig-nes Glück, drohend wohl dem Mörder, freute sich A - ga-thens Lie - bes-blick."

Not only is the poet's verse as such, however, revealed as an absurdity, but, for all the distinctness of its musical phrasing, the *sense* has become extremely difficult to discern. As I was accustomed merely to hearing it sung, it was only after this unintelligibility had one day struck me that I discovered the true sequence of ideas. A similar difficulty arises later in the same aria through the favourite poetic trick of dissociating words for the sake of rhyme. Here the composer unfortunately makes things worse by repeating the parenthesis:

Wenn sich rauschend Blätter regen,
Wähnt sie wohl, es sei mein Fuss
Hüpft vor Freuden, winkt entegen –
Nur dem Laub – nur dem Laub – den Liebesgruss.

When the leaves rustle,
She will know it is my footstep.
Leaping with joy she will wave in my direction –
But her loving greeting is only for the leafy trees.

Moreover 'Fuss' and 'Liebesgruss' are here intended to rhyme. The first time Weber accentuates thus:

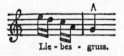

Lie - bes - gruss.

the second time thus:

Lie - bes-gruss.

so that the wrong accent gives the rhyme, but the right accent discloses that these words do *not* rhyme. And so we have a flagrant instance of the utter folly of our whole literary scheme of verse, which almost always rests on end-rhymed lines, though it is only in the finest verses of our greatest and best-reputed poets that the rhyme, through being genuine, is truly effective. Nor has this genuineness or spuriousness much troubled our German composers in the past. To them rhyme was rhyme, and they paired off their last syllables in true street-minstrel fashion. A striking example is offered by Naumann's once-popular melody to Schiller's *Ode to Joy*:

Freude, schöner Götter - fun - ken,   Tochter aus E - ly - si - om,
Wir be - tre - ten feu-er - trun - ken,   Himm-li - sche, dein Hei-ligthum,

Now take Beethoven, the truthful:

Freu-de, schö-ner Göt - ter - fun - ken, Toch-ter aus E - ly - si - um,
Wir be - tre - ten feu - er - trun - ken, Himm-li - sche, dein Hei - ligthum.

For the sake of the imaginary rhyme, Naumann put the verse's accents all askew. Beethoven gave the proper accent, and in doing so, revealed the fact that in German compound words it falls on the first component, so that the end section, bearing the weaker accent, cannot be used for rhyme. If the poet does not adhere to this, the rhyme is present only to the eye, a 'literary' rhyme. It has nothing to offer to the ear, or to the feeling or understanding. And what a complication this wretched rhyme creates in all musical composition to verbal texts: twisting and disfiguring the phrases into utter gibberish, while being not even noticed in the end! In Kaspar's great aria[5] I recently searched for the earlier rhyme to correspond with the last line, 'Triumph, die Rache gelingt', as I had never heard it in the singing, and therefore thought that Weber must have added this clause on his own authority. However, I succeeded in finding 'im Dunkel

[5] In Weber's *Der Freischütz*.

beschwingt', which, hastily strewn between 'umgebt ihn, ihr Geister' and 'schon trägt er knirschend eure Ketten', without any musical caesura, had never struck me as a rhyme before. After all, what use had the composer for this rhyme, when he merely wanted words, or syllables, to give the singer his share in a tempestuous musical phrase that properly belongs to the characteristic orchestral accompaniment alone?

I believe this example, which I selected at random, will afford the best introduction to a further inquiry into the mysteries of operatic melody. The meagre doggerel verse, often built of simply empty phrases, the verse whose sole affinity to music, its rhyme, destroyed the words' last shred of meaning, and thereby made the best images quite valueless to the musician, this verse compelled him to take the pattern and working-out of characteristic melodic motifs from a province of music which had previously been developed in the orchestral accompaniment to a *lingua franca* of the instruments. Mozart had raised this symphonic accompaniment to such expressiveness that, wherever it was consistent with dramatic naturalism, he could let the singers merely speak to it in musical accents, without disturbing the rich melodic texture of themes or breaking up the musical flow. Thus violence towards the verbal text disappeared also. Anything in it that did not call for vocal melody, was clearly intoned. Yet the incomparable dramatic talent of this glorious musician only perfectly accomplished this in so-called *opera buffa*, and only to a lesser degree in *opera seria*. Here his followers were left with a great difficulty. They could see nothing for it but to keep the utterance of passion invariably melodious. Since the threadbare text gave them little help, and wilful repetition of its words had already made them deaf to any claims of the librettist, they finally set the prose part of the text itself, with just as many repetitions as were needed, to melodic-looking phrases such as Mozart had originally assigned to his strongly characterised orchestral accompaniment. Having done this, they thought their singers would always have 'melody' to sing; and to keep it in perpetual motion they often buried all the text, if there was somewhat too much of it, beneath such a mass of scales and runs, that neither song nor text could be discerned. Whoever wants a fairly striking instance should study the Templar's great air in Marschner's *Templar und Jüdin*. Consider the 'allegro furioso' from 'mich fasst die Wuth' onwards, where the composition of the final verses is specially instructive; for in one breath, without the smallest pause, these words stream forth:

> Rache nur wollt' ich geniessen;
> Ihr allein mein Ohr nur leihend
> Trennt' ich mich von allen süssen,
> Zarten Banden der Natur,
> Mich dem Templerorden weihend.

> Vengeance was all I wanted to enjoy;
> Lending my ear to nought else,
> I cast from me all the sweet
> And tender aspects of Nature,
> Consecrating myself to the order of the Templars.

Here the composer pauses, for the poet's having tacked on a 'Bitt're Reue fand ich nur' ('I found only bitter remorse') after the full stop, just to make a rhyme for 'Natur', seemed really too bad. Only after two bars of interlude does Marschner allow this strange addendum to appear, but of course in breathless roulades as before.

Thus the composer believed he had 'melodised' everything. Nor was it better with the elegiac, tender vein, of which the same aria affords us an example in its Andante (3/4): 'in meines Lebens Blüthezeit'. The second verse, 'einsam in das dunkle Grab', is sung in ballad fashion to melodic embellishment which has brought this genre of German vocal music to the verge of the ridiculous. The composer was of the opinion that the singer would always like 'something to sing'. The great bravura fire-works of the Italians did not sparkle so splendidly when at-

tempted by German composers. Only on 'Rache', did Marschner
feel it incumbent on himself to risk a run up and run down.
In the Cantabile, on the contrary, one finds those minor pretti-
nesses, particularly the 'mordente' and its derivative grace-notes,
just to prove that we have taste as well. Spohr brought the
agréments of his violin solos into his singers' arias and if the
melody, apparently composed of these extras, turned out to be
dreary and meaningless, it also strangled the verse that had
been making signs that it had something to say. With Marschner,
in addition to the manifest traits of genius that occur so frequently (in that great Templar aria for instance) and now and
then ascend to positive sublimity (for instance in the choruses
introducing the second finale of the same opera), we meet an
almost overwhelming mawkishness and an often astounding
incorrectness, mostly due to the unfortunate delusion that things
must always go 'melodiously', i.e. must everywhere be tuneful.
My departed colleague Reissiger complained to me of the failure
of his *Schiffbruch der Medusa*, in which, I myself must admit,
there was 'so much melody'. I had to presume this was a bitter
allusion to the success of my own operas, in which, as you
know, there was 'so little melody'.

This wondrous melodic wealth, which emptied its horn of
plenty on the just and unjust alike, made good its squandered
riches by an, alas, not always skilful annexation of all the musical
gimmicks current in the world, mostly filched from French or
Italian operas and carelessly thrown together. Against Rossini
there was many an outcry. Yet it was merely his originality that
vexed us, for as soon as Spohr's violin solo was exhausted at the
end of his Cantabile, Rossini's march and ballet rhythms and
melismata swarmed into the Allegro almost of themselves.
Again, nothing but yards of 'melody'. The overture to the
Felsenmühle still lives on at our garden-concerts and changing
of the guard ceremonies, though it is merely an imitation of the
march from *Mosé*. In this instance German patriotism, to the
great satisfaction of Reissiger's ghost, would seem to have
triumphed.

Yet it was not solely this ineffectual use of Italian and French melismic and rhythmic gimmicks, that cluttered up German operatic melody. It suffered also from the four-part male chorus so passionately practised during the past half-century. Spontini attended a performance of Mendelssohn's *Antigone* in Dresden, against his will; he soon left it with the contemptuous remark: *'C'est de la Berliner Liedertafel!'* It is a sad tale, the incursion of that miserably thin and monotonous beer-chant, even when raised to the rank of a Rhine wine-song, with which even the Berlin composer of the opera *Die Nibelungen* could not dispense. It was the genius of Weber that led the opera into these noble national pathways by introducing into it the German male chorus, to which he had given so splendid an impetus by his songs of the War of Liberation. Its uncommon success encouraged the master to lend its character to the chorus that takes a dramatic part in the action. In his *Euryanthe* the dialogue of the principal characters is repeatedly arrested by the chorus, which unfortunately sings entirely in the strain of the four-part glee, by itself, unrelieved by any characteristic movement in the orchestra, almost as if these passages were intended to be extracted as they stand for the Liedertafel albums. What was most honourably intended by Weber, perhaps in opposition to the stereotyped use of the Italian chorus merely to accompany the aria or ballet, led his successors into that eternal meaningless 'melodic' chorus-work which, together with the aforesaid aria-embellishing, makes up the entire substance of a German opera. Whole scenes are covered by this all-purpose melody, without a single striking moment to tell us the cause of the uninterrupted sea of tunefulness. For an example I return to the operas of that otherwise highly talented Marschner, and point to his so-called ensembles, such as the 'andante con moto' (9/8) in the second finale of his *Templar*, 'Lässt den Shleier mir, ich bitte', and also to the introduction to the first act of the same work, with special reference to the first stanza of the male chorus: 'Wir lagern dort im stillen Wald, der Zug muss hier vorbei, er ist nicht fern, er nahet bald und glaubt die Strasse frei', sung to a hunting-tune; and further on in the opera the extraordinary melodising of dialogue passages with the aid of unimaginable repetitions. Here opera composers may learn how long a large number of men can indulge in an aside on the stage; naturally it can only be done by their standing in rows with their backs to the forest, and facing the audience, which in its turn pays no heed to any of them, but patiently waits for the end of the general 'melody'.

To the intelligent spectator the spoken dialogue in such an opera often comes as a positive relief. On the other hand this very dialogue betrayed composers into the belief that the musical numbers embedded in the prose must always be lyrical in type; an assumption quite justified in the *Singspiel* proper, for there one only wanted vocal intermezzi, while the plot itself was enacted in intelligible prose, just as in a straight play. Here, however, it was opera. The vocal pieces became longer, arias changed places with concerted ensemble numbers, and at last the finale, with all its text, was put at the musician's disposal. And all these separate numbers had to be effective in themselves; their melody was never allowed to flag, and the closing phrase had to be rousing, and applause-provoking. Already the music-dealer had been considered : the more effective, or merely pleasing single pieces that one could extract, the more valuable the work would be to the trade. Even the pianoforte-score had to begin with a table of contents cataloguing the numbers under the rubric of 'Aria', 'Duet', 'Trio', 'Drinking-Song', and so on throughout the whole length of the opera. This continued even when recitative had already ousted the dialogue, and the whole had been given a certain veneer of musical cohesion. To be sure, these recitatives weren't much to speak of, in fact they contributed a great deal to the ennui of the operatic genre. While Nadori in Spohr's *Jessonda*, for instance, delivered himself of the recitative : 'Still lag ich an des Sees Fluthen' –

und las im Ve - da."

one was simply all impatience for the re-entry of the full orchestra with definite tempo and a set 'melody', however badly it might be put together. At the end of these redeeming numbers one had to summon up some applause, the lack of which would eventually have led to the number being omitted.

In the finale, however, quite a tempest of delirium was necessary. A kind of musical orgy was required to bring the act to a satisfying close, so we had an ensemble; every man for himself, all for the audience, and a jubilant burst of melody with a soaring final cadence, appropriate or not, wafted the whole into the appropriate ecstasy. If this also fell flat, the venture had failed, and the opera was withdrawn.

Coupling the above considerations with the utterly chaotic vocalising of most of our singers, their lack of finish aggravated by their absence of style, we must candidly admit that German opera is indeed bungler's work. We must confess this when we compare it with French and Italian opera; but how much more so when we consider the requirements that ought to be met by a drama on the one hand and an independent piece of music on the other, and how little they are met by this pseudo-artwork which incorporates the worst of both worlds! In this opera, in fact, everything becomes absurd, even the original melodies that a gifted musician produces. Weber was a true creator of so-called 'German' opera; he projected his most enkindling rays of genius through this opera-mist, which Beethoven shook off in anger when he wrote in his diary : 'No more operas and suchlike, but *my* way!' Who shall dispute our verdict on the genre itself, when he recalls the fact that Weber's finest, richest and most masterly

music is as good as lost to us because it belongs to the opera
Euryanthe? Where shall we find this work performed today,
when even our kings and emperors are fonder of *Clemenza di
Tito* or *Olympia* – if something heavy must really be dug up
for their wedding or jubilee festivities – than this *Euryanthe*?
And yet, despite the reputation this *Euryanthe* has for tedium,
each single number in it is worth more than all the *opera seria*
of Italy, France and Judaea put together. Such preferences,
beyond a doubt, are not to be simply set down to the somnolent
discrimination of the Prussian Operatic College of Directors. Yet
as everything there is governed by a certain dull but stiff-necked
academic instinct, we may gather from such a choice that beside
those works of undeniably inflexible type, with a very cramped
and hollow style, even the best of German operas must necessarily
look incomplete and therefore unsuitable for presentation at
Court. Certainly all the sins of the operatic genre come out most
strongly in *Euryanthe*, but this is solely because although its
composer was in deadly earnest this time, he could still only
try to cover up the failings and absurdities of the genre by a
supreme exertion of his purely musical faculties. To revive my
old figure of speech, to beget the great complete work of art
in the marriage, the poet's work is the masculine principle,
and music the feminine. I might compare the outcome
of this mingling of the *Euryanthe* text with Weber's genius
with the fruit of the union of a Tschandala with a Brahminess.
According to Hindu belief and experience, a Brahmin might
beget from a Tschandala woman quite a healthy child, though
not one fitted for the rank of Brahmin, whereas the offspring
of a Tschandala male from the superbly truth-bearing womb
of a Brahmin female revealed the low-caste type in its plainest,
and consequently its most revolting form. Moreover at the
conception of this unfortunate *Euryanthe*, you must remember
that the poet-father was a lady, the musician in the fullest sense
a man! When Goethe thought that Rossini could have written
quite passable music for his *Helena*, it was the Brahmin casting
his eye on a buxom Tschandala maiden; only in this case

it is scarcely to be supposed that the Tschandala girl would have stood the test.

In the first part of my larger treatise on 'Opera and Drama'[6] I tried to expound the mournful, indeed heart-rending lessons to be drawn from Weber's last-named work. In particular, I endeavoured to show that even the most richly gifted melodist was in no position to turn a collection of mediocre German verses concocted for a pseudo-poetic operatic text into a first-rate work of art. And Weber, in addition to being one of the most pre-eminent of melodists, was a bright-witted man with a keen eye for all trash and humbug. With the young musicians who came after, he soon fell into disrepute. God knows what mixtures of Bach, Handel and so forth they concocted as the very newest recipes; but none of them ventured to face the problem which Weber seemed to have left unsolved, or, if any did, he quickly gave up after a brief but laboured attempt. Only Kapellmeisters went on gaily composing operas. In their contracts it was written that they must enrich the court opera which they con-ducted with a new product of their imaginations every year. My operas *Rienzi, Der fliegende Holländer, Tannhäuser* and *Lohengrin,* are performed at the Dresden Court Theatre to this day without payment of fee to me, because they are considered as Kapellmeister-operas from the period of my appointment there. I therefore have to pay a curious penalty for these operas having fared better than those of my colleagues. Happily, this calamity affects myself alone. I know of no other Dresden opera composer whose works have survived his period as conductor, except my great predecessor Weber; but they did not ask him to write a work expressly for the Court Theatre, as in his time only Italian opera was deemed compatible with human dignity. Weber wrote his three famous operas for theatres elsewhere.

Apart from my modest works which still, after thirty years, enrich the Royal Saxon Court Theatre's repertoire, not one of the afterbirths of Weberian opera has had any real subsistence

---

[6] *Opera and Drama* comprises Volume 2 (published in 1893) of the English edition of Wagner's prose works.

E

at court theatres. Incomparably the most significant of them were the first operas of Marschner. Untroubled by the problems of opera itself, Marschner was for some time buoyed aloft by the great unrestrainedness with which he gave his melodic talent free rein to work out its own salvation. But the contagion of the new French opera caught him as well, and soon he lost himself irretrievably in the shallows of mediocrity. In the face of Meyerbeer's successes one and all stood silent and abashed, if merely out of good manners. It is only in recent times that composers have dared to follow up with creations in his style, with static subjects drawn from the Old Testament. German opera was on its deathbed until at last it became evident that the still opposed, but less disputed successes of my own works, had pretty well set the whole German world of composition in a state of alarm and eager competition.

Several years ago I noticed symptoms of this movement. My successes at the Dresden Court Theatre had even at that time attracted the interest of Hiller, and later Schumann. At first, no doubt, they merely wanted to discover how it came about that, in an important German theatre the operas of a hitherto entirely unknown German composer could so successfully attract the public. Both friends believed they had soon detected that I was no remarkable musician; so that my success appeared to be founded on the libretti I had written for myself. Indeed I was also of the opinion that, as they were both contemplating operatic composition, they should first of all procure good libretti. For this they solicited my help, but declined it again when things came to the point, presumably for fear of any shabby tricks that I might play on them. Of my libretto for *Lohengrin,* Schumann remarked that it could never be composed as an opera. In this, he differed from Chief Kapellmeister Taubert of Berlin, who later on, after my opera had been completed and performed, declared that he should like to set its libretto to music all over again for himself. When Schumann was compiling the libretto of his *Genoveva* no argument of mine could dissuade him from retaining the lamentably foolish third act as he had framed it. He took offence, and imagined that I wished to spoil his very best effects. For it was effect that he aimed at : everything 'German, chaste and pure', but with a piquant dash of mock unchastity to be harrowingly supplied by the inhuman coarseness and low-nesses of the second finale. A few years ago I heard a carefully prepared performance of this *Genoveva* in Leipzig, and came to the conclusion that the revolting and offensive scene which ends the third act of Auber's *Bal masqué*, which is motivated in the same way, was quite a dainty *bon mot* compared with this sickening brutality by our chaste German effect-composer and librettist. Incredibly, I have never heard a solitary complaint about it. With such energy does the German control his inborn purer feelings when he intends to pit one man, Schumann for instance, against another, e.g. myself. For my part, I perceived that I could have been of no earthly use to Schumann.

But this was in the good old days. After that, the Thirty Years' War of the Music of the Future broke out, as to which I cannot quite ascertain whether the time is yet deemed ripe for a Westphalian treaty. At any rate there was a fair amount of opera composing again in the years of war themselves, prompted perhaps by the very circumstance that our theatres were doing less and less business with the French and Italian wares they used to make their living by, whereas a number of German libretti from my dilettantish pen, and actually composed by my own unaided self, have for some time been furnishing them with good receipts.

Unfortunately, I have been unable to gain any closer acquaint-ance with the creations of the neo-German Muse. They tell me that the influence of my innovations in the dramatic style of music has made its mark. I am widely credited with a style which the deceased Kapellmeitster Rietz of Dresden disliked and at which the late departed Music Director Hauptmann of Leipzig directed his choicest sallies.

I imagine they were not the only ones, and that quite a number of musicians of all sorts were, and probably still are, unfriendly towards this style. In the music schools and conservatoria it is said to be strictly taboo. What style may be taught there is not clear to me. All I know is that precious little is learnt: someone who had studied composition for six whole years at one of these establishments gave it up in the end. It almost seems that the learning of opera composition must proceed in secret, outside the high schools; so that he who falls into my style, had best keep a lookout! But it is less a study of my works, than of their success, that appears to have impelled many an academically untaught composer towards my style. In what this style consists, is not even clear to me. Perhaps my influence can be seen in the recent predilection for medieval subjects. Edda and the rugged North, in general, have also been plundered as quarries for good texts. Yet it is not ony the choice of its opera libretti that seems to have characterised this determinedly 'new' style, but also several other things; in particular that 'composing-throughout', and above all a never ceasing interference of the orchestra into the domain of the singers. A good deal of mannerism has lately arisen in the instrumentation, harmony and modulation of orchestral compositions.

I scarcely think that in all these things I could give much useful instruction. Since, fortunately, I am not asked for it by anyone, at most I might give, unbidden, the following little counsel out of pure good nature.

A German prince with a flair for composing operas once asked the esteemed Liszt to procure my aid in orchestrating a new opera by His Highness. In particular he wanted the fine effect of the trombones in *Tannhäuser* applied to his work, apropos of which my friend Liszt felt bound to divulge the secret that ideas always occurred to me just as I was about to write for the trombones. On the whole it would be advisable for other composers to note the times when their inspiration comes. As to myself, this is of little use, as I can never compose anything when I am not full of ideas; and perhaps most people would be wiser not to wait upon inspiration. With regard to dramatists, however, I would suggest the best method is positively to force such inspiration.

A young musician, whom I also once advised to wait for ideas, asked sceptically how he was ever to know that the idea he might get was really his own. This doubt may also occur to the composer of purely instrumental music : in fact our great symphonic composers of the present time would be well advised to turn any doubt as to the ownership of their random ideas into downright certainty, before others do it for them. A dramatic composer like myself, on the other hand, I would recommend never to think of adopting a text before he is certain it contains a plot, and characters to carry out this plot, that inspire the musician with a lively interest on some account or another. Then let him immediately take a good look at the one character, for instance, which most strongly appeals to him. If it wears a mask, away with it; if it wears the garment of a stage-designer's dummy, off with it! Let him set it in a dimly lighted place, where he can just see the gleaming of its eyes; if that speaks to him, the shape itself will now most likely begin to move. This may even terrify him, but he must put up with that; at last its lips will part, it opens its mouth, and a ghostly voice murmurs something quite distinct and able to be grasped, but so unheard of (such as the Stone Guest,[7] and surely the page Cherubino,[8] speaking to Mozart) that he wakes from his dream. All has vanished; but in the spiritual ear it still rings on : he has had an idea, a so-called musical motif. God knows if other men have heard the same, or something similar, before? Does it please X and Y, or displease Z? What does that matter to him? It is *his* motif, bequeathed to him by that dimly seen shape during those moments of absorption.

But one only gets these inspirations when one keeps aloof from the usual hack librettos, for which it is uncommonly difficult to invent new tunes. We may take it that Mozart has exhausted all the music for those same dramatic masquerades. Clever men have praised his texts, that of *Don Giovanni* for instance, as the half-sketched programmes for a stage masque, with which they

[7] In *Don Giovanni*.
[8] In *Le Nozze di Figaro*.

say his music corresponds so admirably because it reproduces even the most passionate of human situations as a pleasantly diverting game. Though this view is easy to misconstrue and above all may wound as being derogatory, it was seriously meant, and involved that widely accepted verdict of our aesthetes on music's true office which it is so hard to combat even today. I think, however, that Mozart, while elevating this art (exposed, in a certain and very deep sense, to the charge of frivolity) to an aesthetic principle of Beauty, at the same time completely exhausted it. It was his own : whoever attempted to follow him merely bungled everything and bored his listeners.

The stock of attractive melodies has run out and without new ideas there cannot be much originality. Therefore I advise the composer of the latest style to keep a keen eye on his text, his plot and characters, for inspiration. But he who has no time to wait for the results of such a scrutiny and finally contents himself with stage clichés, processions, shrieks of vengeance, and all the dance of death and devils, must be warned. He must not employ for the musical aspect of such barn-storming those attributes of style which have issued from communion with the true dream shapes I spoke of above. If he were to do so, he would only make a muddle of it. For he who has looked those figures in the face, there is a difficulty in drawing on the storehouse of our common-place music to recompense plainly the motif they have given him. Frequently there was nothing to be done with the squaring of rhythm and modulation, since 'It is' means something different from 'Let us say' or 'He believes so'. Here the unknown often necessitates new methods, and the music may perhaps weave itself into a style that might greatly annoy our musical pundits. Not that this matters much : for, if he who makes strange and startling modulations unnecessarily is certainly a bungler, so he who does not recognise the compulsion to modulate forcibly in the proper place is nothing but a politician. The worst of it is, the modern composer assumes that those occasional inspirations have now become the common property of all who have trodden the path, and that if only he lays them on thick enough, his dummies will at once look real. But they look very bad, and I cannot blame many an honest soul of the German Reich for still preferring to hear masque music correctly built according to the lines of quadrature. If only there were Rossinis to be had! I am afraid, however, we have come to the end of them.

There will, after all, not be much to learn from my jottings of today. My advice, in particular, will prove quite useless. Indeed under no circumstances would I pretend to teach how men should create; I wish merely to guide them to a knowledge of how the made and the created should be rightly understood. Even for this a really lasting intercourse is necessary; for only by examples, examples, and again examples, is anything to be made clear, and eventually something learnt. To give effective examples, however, in our domain, we need musicians, singers, finally an orchestra. All these the minions of our Ministries of Culture have at their hands in the schools of the great cities. How they have contrived that nothing right will ever come of our music, that even at the changing of the guard ceremonies the pieces played grow daily worse, must remain a modern mystery of State. My friends are aware that two years ago I thought it would be useful if I involved myself somewhat in this situation. What I wished, however, seemed to be considered undesirable. I have therefore been left in peace, for which I ought to be thankful in some respects. I only regret having to remain so incomplete and hard to understand when I feel moved at times, as with the above, to throw a ray of light on much that touches our world of music. May the present condition be blamed if the present article is found more irritating than instructive : luckily it is not written for either the Cologne, the national or the world newspapers, and whatever is amiss in it thus stays among ourselves.

The Virtuoso and the Artist

Der Virtuose und der Künstler first appeared in a somewhat different French version in the *Revue et Gazette Musicale de Paris* in 1840, and is also to be found, in German, in Volume 1 of the collected works.

*

According to an ancient legend there exists somewhere an inestimable jewel whose shining light bestows forthwith, upon the favoured mortal whose glance rests on it, all spiritual gifts and every joy of a contented spirit. But this treasure lies buried in unfathomed depths. The story goes that the eyes of happy mortals were once blessed with superhuman power to pierce the ruins heaped above it like gateways, pillars, and misshapen fragments of a giant palace: through this chaos there leapt to their sight the wondrous splendour of the magic jewel, which filled their hearts with bliss untold. Then a yearning seized them to remove the pile of wreckage, to unveil to all the world the glory of the magic treasure whose bright rays, putting the sun to shame, should fill our hearts with divine love and our minds with heavenly knowledge. But their every effort was in vain: they could not move the inert mass that hid the wonderful stone.

Centuries passed by: the spirit of those rare and favoured ones still mirrored on the world the radiance of that starry light which had once shone upon them from the glinting jewel; but no one could draw near the jewel itself. Yet tales of it were still told; there were traces, and men conceived the idea of burrowing for the magic stone with all the arts of mining. Shafts were sunk, levels and cross-cuts were driven into the bowels of the earth. The most ingenious of subterranean tactics were employed, fresh mines were dug, and new tunnels constructed, until at last the labyrinth grew so confusing that all remembrance of the right direction was lost for good. And so the whole great maze, the jewel itself having been finally forgotten, lay there uselessly: men gave up all thought of it. The shafts and raises were abandoned: already they were threatening to cave in, when, so it is said, a poor miner from Salzburg passed that way. He carefully surveyed the work of his forerunners: full of astonishment he wandered through the countless mazes, whose useless plan he only half understood. Suddenly, he felt his heart beat faster in sheer rapture: through a chink the jewel blazed forth at him. With one glance he took in the nature of the labyrinth: the longed-for pathway to the magic stone itself grew plain. Led by its light he dived into the deepest cavern, finally to arrive before the heavenly talisman itself. A wondrous radiance then filled the world with fleeting glory, and every heart was thrilled by untold ecstasy: but the miner from Salzburg was never seen again.

Then there came another miner, this time from Bonn in the Siebengebirge, to search in the abandoned levels for the missing Salzburger. He soon found traces of him, and so suddenly did the splendour of the magic jewel smite his eye, that it struck him blind. A foaming sea of light surged through his senses, he flung himself into the chasm, and the timbers crashed down upon him: a fearful din arose, as though a world had foundered. The miner from Bonn was never seen again.

And so, like every miner's story, this ended with a pit falling in. Fresh ruins overlay the old. Yet, to this day, men show the site of the ancient workings, and recently have even begun to dig for the two lost miners, as some kind good people think they might still be alive. With breathless haste the pits are sunk afresh, and are much talked of. The curious come from far and near, to view the spot. Fragments of rock are taken away as souvenirs, and paid for, for everyone would like to have contributed to such a pious work. Moreover, one can buy an account of the two entombed men, which a Bonn professor has carefully drawn up, yet one cannot tell exactly how the accident occurred. And things have finally come to such a pass, that the original legend is completely forgotten, whilst all kinds of minor modern fables take its place, for example that quite prolific veins of gold have been discovered in the diggings, and solid coins struck from them. Indeed there seems to be some truth in this; for people think less and less about the magic stone and those two poor miners, although the whole exploit still has about it the air of a rescue operation.

Perhaps the whole legend, with its subsequent fable, is to be understood in an allegorical sense. On that hypothesis, its meaning would soon be apparent, if we took the magic jewel to be the genius of music. The two incarcerated miners would be no less easy to name, and the debris that covers them would be that which lies under our feet when we prepare ourselves to compete with those enshrined elect. In truth, if he on whom that magic stone has shone in fabled dreams at night, whose soul has felt the fire of music in the holy hours of ecstasy, would fain pursue that dream, that ecstasy (in other words, if he would search for the tools of his trade), he must first of all stumble on that heap of ruins. He has then to dig and delve; the place is filled with gold-diggers; they pile the debris ever higher, and, if you would make for the forgotten shaft, they fling down slag and debris in your way. The rubble grows higher and higher, the wall grows ever thicker : sweat pours in rivers from your brow. Poor fellow! And they laugh at you.

Yet the thing may have a serious side.

What you have written down in notes, is now to be sounded aloud. You want to hear it, and to let others hear it. Very good : the weightiest, nay the ineluctable concern for you, is to get your piece of music brought to realisation exactly as you heard it in your mind when you wrote it down. That is to say, the composer's intentions are to be conscientiously reproduced, so that the thoughts of his spirit may be transmitted unalloyed and undisfigured to the organs of perception. The highest merit of the executant artist, the virtuoso, would accordingly consist in a pure and perfect reproduction of the composer's thought : a reproduction only to be ensured by genuine fathering of his intentions, and consequently by total abstinence from all inventions of one's own. It follows that only a performance directed by the composer in person can give a fine interpretation of his intentions. The next best thing will be a man sufficiently endowed with creative power to gauge the value of observing another artist's intentions by that which he sets upon his own, and it will be an advantage to him to have a certain loving pliability. Then would come such artists as make no claim to productivity, and belong to art, so to speak, merely in virtue of their aptitude for making a stranger's work of art their intimate possession : these would have to be modest enough so entirely to sink their personal attributes, in whatever they may consist, that neither their defects nor their advantages should come to light in the performance. For it is the work of art, purely reproduced, that should step before us, and never the distracting individuality of the performer.

Unfortunately, however, this very reasonable demand runs counter to all the conditions under which artistic products win the favour of the public. The public's first and keenest curiosity is addressed to the performer's skill; delight in that is the only thing which leads to notice of the work itself. Who can blame the public for that? Is it not the very tyrant whose vote we seek to gain? Nor would things stand so badly if this did not end by corrupting the executant artist, and making him finally forget his own true mission. His situation as vehicle of the artistic intention, indeed, as virtual representative of the creative artist, makes it his essential duty to guard the earnestness and purity of art in general : he is the intermediary of the artistic idea, which through him, in a sense, first attains a physical existence. The real dignity of the virtuoso rests, therefore, solely on the dignity he is able to preserve for creative art : if he trifles and toys with this, he casts his own honour away. To be sure, it is of little import to him, should he not have sensed that dignity at all. Although he is not a creative artist, he still has his skills to hand, and these he lets play. They may not warm, but they glitter, and at night it all looks very nice.

There sits the virtuoso in the concert hall, and dazzles us purely on his own behalf : he runs, he jumps; he melts, he pines, he paws and glides, and the audience hangs on his every movement. Go and watch the strange ritual of such a soirée, and try to learn how you should make yourselves presentable for such a gathering. You will find that, of all that passes before your eyes and ears, you understand probably about as much as the performer there understands of what goes on within your soul when music wakes in you and drives you to create. Heavens ! You are to fit your music to suit this man ? Impossible ! At each attempt you would fail miserably. You can swing yourselves into the air, but you cannot dance. A whirlwind lifts you to the clouds, but you can make no pirouette. What would you succeed in, if you took him for your model ? A vulgar catherine-wheel, no more, and everyone would laugh, even if you did not get hurled from the salon.

Plainly we have nothing to do with this virtuoso. But presumably you went to the wrong concert. For indeed there are other virtuosi, and among them true, great artists who owe their reputation to their moving execution of the noblest works of the greatest composers. Where would the public's acquaintance with these latter be, had not those eminently pre-elect arisen from out the chaos of music-making to show the world who the great composers really were and what they had done ? There is the placard, inviting you to such a lordly feast : one name stands out : *Beethoven* ! Enough. Here is the concert hall. And indeed, Beethoven is offered to you. All round sit high-bred ladies, row after row of high-bred ladies, and in a wide half-moon behind them lively gentlemen with lorgnettes held to their eyes. But Beethoven is there, amidst all the perfumed agony of daydreaming elegance : it really is Beethoven, sinewed and broad,

in all his sad omnipotence. But who are those others with him?
Good Heavens! William Tell, Robert the Devil, and who next?
Weber, the tender and true! Good! And then: a galop. O
Lord! Anyone who has ever written galops himself, who has
written his share of pot-pourris, knows what want can drive us to,
when it is a question of approaching Beethoven at all costs. I have
known the measure of the awful need that can still drive a man
today to pot-pourris and galops, to gain the chance of preaching
Beethoven; and though I must admire the virtuoso in this instance, I cursed all virtuosity. So falter not, true disciples of art,
upon the path of virtue. If a magic power drew you to dig for the
silted shaft, be not misguided by those veins of gold; but delve
deeper, ever deeper towards the magic stone. My heart tells me
that those buried miners are living yet. If not, then believe it in
any case. The belief will do you no harm.

But is it all mere foppery? You need the virtuoso, and, if he's
the right sort, he needs you too. At least, that's how it must once
have been. For something happened to cause a division between
the virtuoso and the artist. In former times it was certainly
easier to be one's own virtuoso; but artists became overambitious,
and wrote works so difficult to perform that they were obliged
to turn their execution over to men who have to devote their
whole lives to performing the works of others' labour. Indeed
you should be grateful to the virtuoso. He is the first to face
the tyrannical public: if he doesn't perform his task well, nobody
asks about your composition, but *he* is hissed off the boards. Can
you be cross with him then, if, when applauded, he takes that for
himself, and does not specially return his thanks in the name of
the composer? Nor would that be quite what you want: you want
your piece performed precisely as you conceived it. The virtuoso
is to add nothing to it, leave nothing out of it; he is to be your
second self. But often that is very hard. Let one of you just try, for
once, to sink himself so entirely in the work of another!

Consider the man who certainly thinks least about himself, and
to whom the personal act of pleasing has surely nothing special
to bring in, the man who conducts an orchestra. He surely fancies

he has penetrated to the very soul of the composer, indeed that he has drawn him on like a second skin? You can't tell me that *he* is behaving like an upstart when he takes your tempo wrong, misunderstands your expression-marks, and drives you to desperation when you hear your own composition. Yet he can be a virtuoso too, and tempt the public by all kinds of spicy nuances into thinking that, after all, it is he who makes the whole thing sound so nice. He finds it pleasing to let a loud passage be played quite soft, for a change, and a fast one a trifle slower; he will add, here and there, a trombone-effect, or a dash of the cymbals and triangle; but his chief resource is to make a drastic cut, if he has no other method of ensuring success. Him we must call a virtuoso of the baton; and I fancy he's none too rare, especially in opera houses. So we shall have to arm ourselves against him; and the best way will probably be to ally ourselves with the real and original, not second-hand virtuoso – the singer.

Now, the composer so thoroughly impregnates the singer, that his music streams from the performer's throat as living tone. Here, one would think, no misunderstanding is possible : the virtuoso performer has to make his choice, and he may choose the wrong thing; but there, in the singer, we are left with the melody itself. It will certainly be unfortunate, if our melody is not emanating from the right part of him. He, too, has approached us from outside : have we got down as far as his heart, or simply stuck in his throat? We were digging for the jewel in the depths : are we caught in the toils of the gold-veins.

The human voice, also, is an instrument; it is rare, and paid for dearly. How it is shaped, is the first concern of the inquisitive public, and next, how it is played upon. What it plays is immaterial to most listeners. The singer knows better : for what he sings must be so formed as to make it easy for him to play on his voice to best advantage. How small, in comparison, is the attention the virtuoso needs to give to his instrument. It stands there ready made; if it suffers harm, he gets it repaired. But this priceless, wondrously capricious instrument of the voice? No man quite understands its structure. Write what you please you composers, but take care that it is something the singer enjoys singing. How are you to set about it? Why, go to concerts, or better still, to salons! You don't want to write for these, but for the theatre, the opera, dramatic music? Good! Then go to the opera, and discover that you are still merely in the salon, the concert hall. Here, too, it is the virtuoso with whom you must first come to terms. And this virtuoso, believe me, is more perilous than all the rest; for wherever you meet him, he'll slip through your fingers.

Consider the most celebrated singers in the world: from whom would you learn, if not from the artists of our great Italian opera, who are worshipped as positively superhuman beings, not only in Paris, but in every capital of the world? Here you may learn what really is the art of song. From them the famous singers of the French Grand Opéra first learnt what singing means. They learnt that there is more to it than is dreamed of by our German scrape-throats who think all is well if their heart is in the right place, namely seated tight upon their stomach. There you will meet also the composers who understood how to write for real singers. They knew that only through these singers could they arrive at recognition, or even exist; and as you see, they are there, doing well, honoured and glorified. But you don't want to compose for singers? Your works are to be respected for themselves? It is from great music that you will take your cue, not from the success of the vocal feats of the singers to whom those others owe their fortune? Look a little closer: have these singers no passion? Do they not tremble and heave, as well as lisp and gurgle? When they sing 'Ah! Tremate!' it sounds somewhat different from your 'Zittre, feiger Bösewicht!' Have you forgotten that 'Maledetta!' at which the best-bred audiences turned into a negro revivalist meeting? But to you it doesn't seem the genuine thing? You think it a parcel of effects, at which all reasonable men should laugh?

However, this also is art, and one which these celebrated singers have carried far. With the singing-voice, too, one may toy and juggle as one pleases; but the game must finally be related to some passion, for one does not otherwise need to pass from rational talk to the decidedly much louder noise of singing. Ah! now you have it: the public wants an emotion it cannot get at home like whist or dominoes. This, also, may have been quite different at one time. Great masters found great pupils among their singers; the tradition still lives of the wonderful things they brought to life together, and it is often renewed by fresh experience. Most certainly one knows and demands that song should also work dramatically, and our singers therefore learn so thorough a command of passion that it looks as if they had never been without it. And its use is very well regulated. After a lot of cooing and chirping, an explosion makes a quite un-paralleled effect. Its not being an actual matter of fact, is just what makes it art.

You still have scruples, founded principally on your contempt for the sickly stuff those singers sing. From whence does it spring? Precisely from the will of those singers, on whose behalf it is cobbled up. What in the world can a true musician wish to have in common with this handiwork? But how would it be if these fêted demigods of the Italian opera were to undertake a real work of art? Are they capable of really catching fire? Can they bear the bright lightings of that magical jewel's flame?

Look, *Don Giovanni*! By Mozart! Thus reads the poster for today.

Actually, strange things happened to me, when I heard *Don Giovanni* recently with great Italian singers. It was a chaos of every sensation in which I was trundled to and fro; for I really found the perfect artist, but close beside him the most absurd virtuoso, who did his best to obstruct him. Grisi[1] as Donna Anna was glorious, and Lablache as Leporello was unsurpassable. The great, richly-gifted Grisi was inspired with but one thought:

---

[1] Giulia Grisi (1811-69), soprano, was one of the most renowned singers of her time. She appeared frequently in operas with the equally celebrated singers Luigi Lablache (1794-1858), bass, Antonio Tamburini (1800-76), baritone, and Giovanni Rubini (1795-1854), tenor.

to be Mozart's own Donna Anna. Everything about her was warmth and tenderness, fire, passion, grief and despair. She knew that the buried miner is still living, and blessedly she fortified my own belief. But the silly soul consumed herself for Signor Tamburini, the world-famous baritone who sang and played Don Giovanni. The entire evening, the man could not rid himself of the shackles that were tied to his legs with this fatal role. I had previously heard him in an opera of Bellini's : there we had 'Tremate', 'Maledetta', and all the passion of Italy rolled into one. Nothing of the sort today : the brief swift pieces whizzed past him like fugitive shadows; much airy recitative all stiff and flat; a fish out of his element. But it seemed that the whole audience was out of its element too. It remained so decorous that one could detect no sign of the usual frenzy. Perhaps a worthy mark of homage to the true genius whose spirit was manifest tonight throughout the theatre? We shall see. In any case the divine Grisi herself was not at her most entrancing. Nobody could quite appreciate her secret passion for this tiresome Don Giovanni. But there was also Lablache, a colossus, and yet tonight every inch a Leporello. How did he manage it? The enormous bass voice sang throughout in the clearest, most superb of tones, and yet it was more like a chattering, babbling, saucy, laughing, hare-footed scampering. On one occasion he reduced his voice to falsetto, and yet it always sounded full, like distant church-bells. He neither stood nor walked, nor did he dance; but he was always in motion. One saw him here, there, everywhere, and yet he never fidgeted. He was always on the spot, before you knew it, wherever a fine sense of humour could scent out fun or frolic in the situation. Lablache was not applauded once in all the evening. That might be understandable, a token of dramatic taste in the audience. But the latter seemed really annoyed that its authorised favourite, Madame Persiani (one's heart convulses at the mere mention of that name!), was ill at ease in the music for Zerlina. I perceived that everyone was prepared to be charmed beyond all bounds with her, and whoever had heard her a short while before in *L'elisir d'amore* could not be blamed for this predilection. But Mozart was decidedly to blame, that the charm refused to work tonight. More dry land, for such a lively fish! Ah! what would not audience and Persiani have given today, had it been thought fitting to infuse a few drops from that 'Elixir of Love'! In fact, I gradually noticed that both sides were bent on an excess of decency: there reigned a unanimity which I was a long time in accounting for. Why, since to all appearance one was 'classically' minded, did the magnificent and perfect execution of the glorious Donna Anna not carry everyone into that sterling ecstasy which seemed to be the only decent state to be in? Why, since strictly speaking one felt ashamed of being carried away, had one come to a performance of *Don Giovanni* at all? Truly the whole evening seemed a voluntary act of penance, imposed on oneself for some unknown reason. But to what end? Something must really be gained by it; for such a Paris audience will spend much, it's true, but always expects a return for its money, even if it's only a worthless one.

This riddle solved itself too : Rubini fired off in the course of this evening his famous trill from A to B! The whole thing came to me in a flash. How could I have expected anything much from poor Don Ottavio, the frequently mocked tenor-stopgap of Don Giovanni? Indeed, for much of the evening I felt truly sorry for the so unreservedly adored Rubini, the wonder of all tenors, who for his part attacked his Mozart role with a distinct lack of enthusiasm. There he came, the sober, solid man, passionately dragged in by the arm by the divine Donna Anna, and stood with ruffled peace of mind beside the corpse of his father-in-law to be, who now no more could breathe his blessing on a happy marriage. Some say that Rubini was once a tailor, and looks just like one; I should have expected him to display more agility in that case : where he stood he stayed, and moved no farther; for he could sing, too, without stirring a muscle. Even his hand was moved but seldom to the region of his heart. This time his singing was never at all moving. He sounded as though he was saving his fairly aged voice for something better than crying out words of comfort, already heard a thousand times, to his beloved. That seemed reasonable, and I thought the man sensible. As he took the same course throughout the opera whenever he was on stage, I fancied at last that that was that, and found myself wondering how he had been induced to accept the role. Then slowly came a stir: unrest, sitting-up, shrewd glances, fan-play, all the symptoms of a sudden straining of attention in a cultured audience. Ottavio was now alone on the stage; I thought he was about to make an announcement, for he came right up to the prompter's box: but there he stayed, and listened without moving a feature to the orchestral prelude to his B flat aria. This 'ritornello' seemed to last longer than usual, but that was a simple illusion; the singer was merely lisping out the first ten bars of his song so utterly inaudibly that, on my discovering that he really looked as though he was singing, I thought the genial man was playing a joke. Yet the audience kept a serious face, for it knew what was coming. At the eleventh bar Rubini let his F swell out with such a sudden vehemence that it struck us like a thunderbolt, and died away again into a murmur with the twelfth bar. I could have laughed aloud, but the whole house was still as death. A muted orchestra, an inaudible tenor; the sweat stood on my brow. Something monstrous seemed to be in preparation, and truly the unhearable was now to be eclipsed by the unheard-of. The seventeenth bar arrived: here the singer has to hold an F for three bars long. What can one do with a simple F? Rubini only becomes divine on the high B flat: that's where he has to get to, if a night at the Italian opera is to have any sense. And just as the trapezist swings his bar in a preliminary movement, so Don Ottavio mounts his three-barred F, two bars of which he gives in careful but pronounced crescendo, till at the third he snatches from the violins their trill on A, shakes it himself with waxing vehemence, and at the fourth bar sits in triumph on the high B flat, as if it were nothing. Then, with a brilliant roulade, he plunges down again, before us all, into his customary silence. The end had come: anything might happen now. Every demon was unchained, and not on the stage, as at the close of the opera, but in the audience. The riddle was solved: this was the trick for which people had assembled, for which they had put up with two hours of total abstinence from every expected operatic dainty, had pardoned Grisi and Lablache for taking such music in earnest, and for which they now felt richly rewarded, with this one wondrous moment when Rubini leapt to B flat!

A German poet once assured me that, in spite of it all, the French were the true Greeks of our era, and that the Parisians in particular had something Athenian about them; for really it was they who had the keenest sense of form. This came back to me that evening. It was true that this uncommonly elegant audience showed not a spark of interest in the score of *Don Giovanni*; to them it was plainly something on which the drapery of unrivalled virtuosity had first to be hung, to give the music its formal right to existence. But Rubini alone could do this properly, and so it was easy to guess why this cold and venerable being had become the darling of the Parisians, the idol worshipped by all cultivated friends of song. In their predilection for this virtuoso aspect of things they go so far as to give this their whole aesthetic interest, while their feeling for noble warmth, even for manifest beauty, cools down more and more. Without one genuine throb they saw and heard that noble Grisi, the splendid woman with the soulful voice. Perhaps they fancy it too realistic. But Rubini, the broad-built Philistine with bushy whiskers, old, with a voice grown greasy, and afraid of over-taxing it: if he is ranked above all others, the charm can hardly reside in his substance, but purely in a spiritual form. And this form is forced upon every singer in Paris: they all sing *à la* Rubini. The rule is: be inaudible for a while, then suddenly alarm the audience by a husbanded explosion, and immediately afterwards relapse into a ventriloquist effect. Duprez already tends to obey this rule. I have often searched for the substitute, hidden somewhere beneath the podium like the mother's-voice trumpet in *Robert the Devil,* that seemed to take the part of the ostensible singer at the prompter's box, who now appeared not to be singing. But that is 'art'. What do we blockheads know about it? Taken all in all, that Italian performance of *Don Giovanni* has consoled me greatly. There really are great artists among the virtuosi, or, to put it another way, even the virtuoso can be a great artist. Unfortunately they are so entangled with each other, that it is a sorrowful task to sift them out. That evening Lablache and Grisi distressed me, while Rubini diverted me hugely. Is there something corrupting, then, in setting these great differences side by side? The human heart is so evil, and hebetude so very sweet! Take care how you play with the Devil! He'll come at last when you least expect him. That's what happened to Signor Tamburini as Don Giovanni that evening, where he surely would never have expected it. Rubini had happily swung himself up to his high B flat: simperingly, he looked down quite amiably upon the Devil. I thought to myself: my God, if the Devil would only take Rubini!

Presumptuous thought! The whole audience would have plunged to Hell after him.

(To be continued in the next world!)

The Wibelungen:
World History as Told in Saga

Die Wibelungen, published as a pamphlet in 1849, was written in the summer of 1848. In that same summer, Wagner made his first prose sketches of the Nibelungen myth as the basis of a music drama. This was eventually, of course, to become *The Ring*. *Die Wibelungen* also appears in Volume 2 of the collected works.

*

THE ANCIENT KNIGHTHOOD

Their coming from the East has lingered on in the memory of European peoples down through the ages: sagas preserved this recollection, however much it became distorted. The maintenance of kingly power among the different nations, its restriction to one favoured race, the fidelity with which it was accorded solely to that race even in the latter's deepest degeneracy, must have had a deep foundation in the people's consciousness: it rested on the memory of their original Asiatic home,[1] on the origin of races from one family, and on the might of the family's head, the tribal father 'sprung from the gods'.

To gain a true conception of this, we must think of those peoples somewhat as follows.

At the epoch which most sagas call the Flood or Great Deluge,

[1] Wagner uses the term 'Urkönigthum', and also 'Urheimath', 'Ursagen' and so on, when referring to these ancient races and their customs. ('Ur-' meaning primitive or original.)

when our earth's northern hemisphere was almost as much covered by water as the southern is now, the largest island of this northern world sea would have been the highest mountain range of Asia, the so-called Indian Caucasus. Upon this island – these mountains – we have to seek the cradle of the present Asiatic peoples, and of those who swept through Europe. Here is the ancestral seat of all religions, of every tongue, of the kinghood of all these nations.

But the original kinghood was the patriarchate: the father was the bringer-up and teacher of his children. To them his discipline and doctrine seemed the power and wisdom of a higher being, and the larger the family grew, the more prolific in collateral branches, the more peculiar and divine must the mould of its original head have seemed, to whom the family owed not only its body, but also all its spiritual life and customs. As this head laid down both discipline and doctrine, the royal and priestly powers were naturally united in him, and his authority was bound to grow in proportion as the family became a race. Moreover, as his power was transferred to his direct heirs, the tribe recognised these as their chieftains, and finally, the long-deceased father of the race, from whom undisputed honour flowed, appeared to them to be a god, or at least the earthly avatar of an ideal god. This idea in turn, consecrated by time, could only serve to perpetuate the fame of that original race whose direct descendants formed the chieftains of the day.

Now, when the waters retreated from the northern hemisphere to flood the southern one again, and the earth thus took on its present guise, the teeming population of that mountain isle descended to the new-found valleys, the gradually emerging plains. The reasons for the hardening of the patriarchate into a monarchic despotism among the races living in the broad and fruitful plains of Asia, have been sufficiently touched on. The races wandering farther westwards, and eventually reaching Europe, began a livelier and freer evolution. Constant war and want in rawer climates and regions frequently brought forth the feeling and the consciousness of independence, in members of the tribe, with the immediate result of the formation of the community. Every head of a family exerted his power over his nearest kin in the same way that the chieftain claimed the right of ancient usage over the clan. In the bond between all the heads of families the king thus found his counterpart, and finally his limitation. The important factor, however, was that the king soon lost his priestly office, the right to interpret God's decree – the manifestation of God – since this was now fulfilled for the immediate family by its head with the same authority as the tribal father had fulfilled it for his tribal family. The king was accordingly left with little more power than that which ensured his godlike decrees should be executed, as interpreted by the members of the community, in the equal interest of all, and in accordance with the customs of the tribe. But the more the community was busied with ideas of worldly right, with property and the individual's right to its enjoyment, the more that vision of God, which had originally ranked as an essentially higher prerogative of the chieftain, tended to give way to a personal verdict in secular matters. Consequently the religious element of the patriarchate dwindled more and more. However, a feeling of reverence still clung to the person of the king and his immediate kinsmen. He was the visible point of union; in him the clan saw the successor to the original father of the widely-branching tribe, and in each member of his family was the purest of that blood from which the whole race had sprung. Though even this idea grew dim in time, awe and honour of the royal line dwelt ever more deeply in the people's heart the more incomprehensible the reason for the original distinction of this house became, and the sole unchanged tradition decreed that from no other line must its kings be chosen. We find this in almost all the races that migrated into Europe, and plainly recognise its bearing on the tribal kings of Greek pre-history. It manifests itself most clearly, however, in the German clans, and above all in the ancient royal lineage of the Franks, who, under the name of the 'Wibelingen' or 'Gibelinen', advanced an age-old royal claim to world dominion.

The Frankish royal line makes its first appearance in history under the name of 'Merovingians': we know that, even in the deepest degeneration of this line, it never occurred to the Franks to choose their kings from any other. Every male member of this family was competent to rule; if men could not tolerate the vices of one, they sided with another, but never left the family itself. This was at a time of such corruption of the national code through the acceptance of the Roman taint that almost every noble family had adopted alien customs, so that the race could hardly have been recognised without its royal line. It was as if the people knew that, without this royal stem, it would cease to be the Frankish race. The idea of the inalienable title of this race must therefore have been deeply rooted, and it was only after centuries of fearful struggles and when it had reached its highest ideal state, and then afterwards declined, that the race decayed, and with its death begins a wholly new ordering of the world. This was the downfall of the 'Ghibellines'.

THE NIBELUNGEN

The ceaseless striving of men and races towards unattainable goals will find a clearer explanation in their primeval racial sagas than in the bare facts of history, which tell us only the consequences of their actions. If we read the saga of the Frankish royal race aright, we find therein a much clearer explanation of its historic deeds than that which we can find elsewhere.

Unquestionably the *Saga of the Nibelungen* is the birthright of the Frankish race. Research has shown the basis of this saga, too, to be of a religio-mythical nature. Its deepest meaning was the conscience of the Frankish race, the soul of its royal line, regardless of the name first given to that race in the primal Asiatic highlands.

For the moment we will not bother with the oldest meaning of the myth, in which we shall recognise Siegfried as the God of Light – or Sungod. To trace its connection with history, we will merely take the saga where it clothes itself with the more human garb of the ancient heroes. Here we find Siegfried as the winner of the Nibelung's Hoard and, with it, of immeasurable might. This Hoard, and the power residing in it, becomes the immovable centre round which all further shaping of the saga now revolves. The whole drama and struggle is aimed at this Hoard of the Nibelungen, as the epitome of earthly power, and he who owns it, who governs by it, either is or becomes a Nibelung.

Now the Franks, whom we first meet in history in the region of the Lower Rhine, have a royal line in which appears the name 'Nibelung'. This occurs especially among its purest branches who, even before the time of Clovis, were ousted by a kinsman, Merovech,[2] but regained the kingship later as Pepins or Carlovingians. Let this suffice for the present, to show, if not the genealogical, at least the mythical identity of the Frankish royal family with those Nibelungen of the saga. The saga has adopted unmistakable features from the history of this race into its later, more historical development, where the focus is still upon possession of that Hoard, the cynosure of earthly rulers.

After the founding of their reign in Roman Gaul, the Frankish kings attacked and overthrew the other German clans, the Allemani, Bavarians, Thuringians and Saxons. Consequently, the latter henceforth bore the relation of subjects to the Franks, and, though their tribal usages were mostly left in fact, they had to suffer the indignity of being totally robbed of their royal houses, in so far as these had not already disappeared. This loss brought home to them the full extent of their dependence, and in the deprivation of its symbol they mourned the downfall of their native freedom. Though the heroic lustre of Charlemagne, in whose might the germ of the Nibelungen Hoard appeared to reach its fullest force, diverted for some time the German races' deep discontent, and made them gradually forget the fame of their own dynasties, yet their loathing never completely

---

[2] Merovech, who succeeded Clodio in the middle of the fifth century, became a legendary figure. He was the grandfather of Clovis (481-511), the true founder of the Frankish monarchy.

vanished. Under Charlemagne's successors it leapt so strongly
back into force that the division of the great Empire and the
severance therefrom of a united Germany, must be mainly at-
tributed to the struggle of the downtrodden German races for
freedom from the Frankish rule. A total severance from domination by the Frankish dynasty, however, was not to take place
until much later; for, though the purely German races were now
united in one independent kingdom, yet the bond of this union
of earlier autonomous and severed national stems still consisted
in the kingly function, and this could only be unjustly claimed by
a member of that original Frankish race. The whole inner
movement of Germany therefore made for independence of the
separate races under new derivatives of old clans, a process
accelerated by the annulment of the unifying royal power exerted
by the hated foreign race.

With the death of the last male Carlovingian[3] in Germany
we are consequently brought to the point when a total sundering
of the German races was almost achieved, and would surely have
been realised, had there still existed any plainer vestiges of the
ancient royal dynasties of the single races. The German Church
in the person of its virtual patriarch, the Archbishop of Mainz,
then saved the tottering unity of the Empire by delivering the
royal authority to Duke Conrad von Franken, who likewise
sprang, on the female side, from the ancient race of kings. But the
weakness of his rule again brought the inevitable reaction, as is
shown in the attempt to choose a king from among the strongest
of the earlier subject German races, now no longer manageable.

The fact that his race was also connected by marriage with the
Carlovingians may have counted in the choice of the Saxon
Duke Henry. But the resistance the whole new Saxon royal
house had constantly to combat is evident from the mere fact that
the Franks and Lothringians, that is those peoples who numbered
themselves with the original ruling dynasty, would never recognise as lawful king the scion of a race once conquered by them,

[3] In 987.

whilst the other German races felt just as little desire to pay allegiance to a king imposed upon them by a people no more powerful than their own, and equally subjected by the Franks in former times. Otto I was the first to subdue the whole of Germany, chiefly because he aroused the national feeling of the Allemani and Bavarians – German races – against the violent and proud hostility of the strictly Frankish races. The combination of their interests with his kingly ambition supplied the force to crush the old Frankish pretensions. The consolidation of his sovereignty, however, appears to have been greatly helped by his attainment of the Roman Emperorship, renewed in former days by Charlemagne, for this conferred on him the lustre of the old Frankish ruling house, which still compelled respect. As if his family had plainly seen this, his successors made incessant journeys to Rome and Italy, returning with that halo of reverence so evidently intended to veil their native lineage in oblivion and translate them to the rank of that original race alone equipped to rule. They thus had won the 'Hoard' and turned to 'Nibelungen'.

The century of kingship of the Saxon house, however, forms a relatively short interregnum in the infinitely longer empire of the Frankish clan. After the extinction of the Saxon house, the royal power returned to a scion of that Frankish race, Conrad the Salier, in whom again a female kinship with the Carlovingians was proved and respected, and the power remained with this house until the downfall of the 'Ghibellines'. The choice of Lothair of Saxony, between the extinction of the male Frankish stem and its continuation by descendants on the distaff side, the Hohenstaufen, may be deemed a mere reactionary attempt, and this time of little durability. Still more so was the later choice of the Guelph Otto IV. Only with the beheading of young Conrad at Naples can the ancient royal race of the 'Wibelingen' be regarded as totally extinct. Strictly speaking, we must recognise that after him there were no more German kings, and still less emperors, in the ideal sense of that term amongst the Wibelingen.

WIBELINGEN OR WIBELUNGEN

The name Ghibellines (Wibelingen), designating the emperor's faction in opposition to the Guelfs (or Guelphs), is of frequent occurrence, especially in Italy, where the two opposing factions were most active. Upon a closer examination, however, we find how utterly impossible it is to explain these highly significant names by historical documents. And this is natural : the bare facts of history scarcely ever offer us, and always incompletely, the material for an explanation of the inmost (so to speak instinctive) motives of the ceaseless struggles of peoples and races. That we must seek in religion and saga, where we shall find it convincingly and clearly revealed.

Religion and saga are the significant products of the people's insight into the nature of things and men. From olden times people have had the inimitable faculty of seizing their own essence according to the generic idea, and plainly reproducing it in plastic personification. The gods and heroes of their religion and saga are the concrete personalities in which the folk spirit reveals itself. However sharply delineated the individuality of these personages, they are of the most universal, all-embracing type, and therefore these shapes have a strangely lasting life. Since every new direction of the people's nature can be gradually imparted to them, they are always in the mood to suit it. Hence the people are thoroughly sincere and truthful in their stories and inventions, whereas the learned historian who is guided by pragmatism and surface events, without regard to the direct expression of the people's bond of solidarity, is pedantically untrue because he is unable to understand intimately the very subject of his work, and therefore he is unconsciously driven to arbitrary subjective speculations. The people alone understand the people, because each day and hour they perform and consummate that which by their very essence they both can and should perform; whereas their learned schoolmasters cudgel their heads in vain to comprehend what the people do instinctively.

If, to prove the truthfulness of the people's insight with reference to our present case, instead of a history of lords and princes we had a folk-history, we should certainly also find in it that the German peoples always had a name for that wondrous Frankish race of kings which filled them all with awe and reverence of a special kind : a name we finally discover again in history, disguised in Italian as 'Ghibelini'. That this name applied not only to the Hohenstaufen in Italy, but was also given to their forerunners in Germany, the Frankish emperors, is historically attested by Otto von Freisingen : the current form of this name in the Upper Germany of his time was 'Wibelingen' or 'Wibelungen'. Now this title would entirely conform with the name of the chief heroes of the Frankish saga, as also with the demonstrably frequent family name among the Franks, of Nibeling, if the change of the initial letter N to W could be accounted for. The linguistic difficulty can easily be overcome, if we consider the origin of just that consonantal change. This lay in the people's speech, which, following the German idiom's native bent, made an alliteration of the two opposing parties, Welfs and Nibelungs, and gave the preference to the party of German origin by placing the name of the 'Welfen' first and making that of the foes of their independence come after it as a rhyme. 'Welfen und Wibelungen' were for many ages known and named by the people, long before it ever occurred to learned chroniclers to plague themselves with the derivation of these, to them, recondite popular nicknames. The Italian people, likewise standing nearer to the Welfs in their feud against the emperors, adopted these names from the German oral tradition, and allowed their dialect to change them into 'Guelphi' and 'Ghibelini'. But Bishop Otto of Freisingen was inspired by a learned error to derive the title of the emperor's faction from the name of a wholly irrelevant village, Waiblingen; a charming foible that plainly proves how unfit scholars are to understand phenomena of world-historical import, such as these immortal names handed down by oral tradition. The Swabians knew better who the

'Wibelungen' were, for, from the time of the ascendence of their blood-related Welfs, they gave this name to the Nibelungen.

If we borrow from the people its conviction of the identity of this name with that of the ancient Frankish dynasty, an exact and intimate understanding of this race's wondrous strivings and ambitions, as also of the doings of its physical and spiritual opponents, becomes so clear that we are enabled to look into the mainsprings of one of the most eventful periods of historical evolution with a clearer eye and fuller heart than our dry-as-dust chronicles can ever give us. In that mighty Nibelungen saga we are shown the race as if it were the embryo of a plant, whose natural conditions of growth, of fruition and death, are clearly revealed to the attentive observer.

So let us embrace that conviction. We must hold it as fervently as it was held in the minds of the people of the Middle Ages, together with the deeds of that famous race, until the poetic literature of the Hohenstaufen period, when we may plainly distinguish in the chivalrous poems of Christianity the Welfian element, now becoming religious in tone, and, in the newly-furbished *Nibelungenlieder,* the utterly contrasting Wibelingian principle with its still pagan outline.

THE WELFEN

Before proceeding to a closer examination of the above, it is necessary to define more clearly the direct opponents of the Wibelingen, the party of the Welfen. In the German language 'Welfe' means sucklings, principally of dogs, but also of quadrupeds in general. The notion of pure descent and nurture at the mother's breast was easily conjoined to this, and in the poetic folk-language a 'whelp' would soon be tantamount to a purebred son, born and suckled by the lawful mother.

In the times of the Carlovingians, there enters a race in which the name of *Welf* is handed down to later generations. It is a Welf who first arrests the course of history by declining to ally himself with the Frankish kings. As he could not stop his sons from entering upon relationships, partly connubial and partly feudal, with the Carlovingians, the old father left his lands in deep disgust and withdrew into the wilderness, so as not to witness his race's shame.

If the dry chronicles of that time bothered to record this trait, to them so unimportant, we may certainly assume that it was far more actively embraced and spread abroad by the people of the downtrodden German races; for this incident, whose like may have often occurred before, expressed with energy the proud yet suffering self-consciousness of all the German races opposed to the ruling tribe. *Welf* may thus have been acclaimed a 'true whelp', a genuine son of the true female line; and, with the constantly increasing wealth and honour of his race, it could easily end in the name *Welf* being viewed by the people as synonymous with German tribal independence against the often feared but never beloved Frankish sovereignty.

In Swabia, their ancestral seat, the Welfs finally beheld a fresh shame brought upon them by the advancement of the petty Hohenstaufens through intermarriage with the Frankish emperors and the winning of the status of Swabian, and thereafter Frankish dukes. King Lothair used their natural bitterness against this race as the chief means of resistance to the Wibelungen, who openly impugned his royal right. He increased the power of the Welfs to a degree previously unknown by granting them simultaneously the two dukedoms of Saxony and Bavaria. It was only through the assistance thus obtained that it became possible for him to assert his kingship against the clamour of the Wibelungen; and indeed, to humble them so that they decided to found a future stronghold among the German peoples by intermarriage with the Welfs. The possession of the major part of Germany increasingly fell to the Welfen; and, though his Wibeling predecessors had deemed it expedient to withdraw it from them, Frederick I appears to have seen in the recognition of such an estate the surest means of reconcilement with an invincible national party, and the way to lay at last the hatred of ages. In a sense, he pacified them by material possessions, thus making it easier for himself to realise his own ideal of the empire which he conceived more clearly than his predecessors had done.

The part which the Welfs played in the final downfall of the Wibelungen, and with them of the stricter German monarchy, is plainly told in history. The latter half of the thirteenth century shows us the final stages of reaction of the narrower national spirit of the German races, in their thirst for independence, against the royal yoke originally imposed upon all by the Franks. That these races were almost entirely disunited internally until then, is to be explained, among other things, by their having lost their royal families as a result of their first subjection to the Franks. Their old noble houses, the next of kin to the former, could therefore more easily make themselves absolute under the shelter and pretext of inherited imperial fiefs, and thus induce the thorough dispersal of the races in whose broader national interest the fight against the supremacy of the Wibelungen had initially been waged. The ultimately successful reaction was therefore founded less upon an actual triumph of the races, than on the collapse of the central kingly power undermined by that fight. That it did not take place in the interest of the people themselves, but in the interest of lords who were splitting up the old clans, is thus an ugly feature of this historical evolution, however much the result had its origins in the existing historic elements themselves. We may call everything related hereto the 'Welfic' principle (regardless of any saga), in opposition to that of the Wibelungen, which developed into nothing less than a claim to world-dominion.

F

THE NIBELUNGEN HOARD IN THE FRANKISH
ROYAL RACE

In order to grasp clearly the inner relation of the Nibelungen saga to the historical significance of the Frankish kingship, let us consider in more detail the historic doings of this ancient princely race.

We cannot ascertain for certain the state of inner dissolution of the tribal system among the Frankish races when they at last arrived at their home, the present Netherlands. We at first distinguish Salic and Ripuarian Franks; and it is not merely this distinction, but also the fact that larger districts had their independent princes, that makes it obvious that the original kingship had become more democratic through the breaking away and also the later re-uniting of branch-races. One thing is certain, that kings or commanders were only chosen from the members of the original dynasty of the race: their power over the other clans was evidently hereditary. Although a chief of all the assembled branches was chosen for great enterprises held in common, it could only be, as mentioned above, from the line of the primeval race of kings.

In 'Nibelgau' we see established undoubtedly the oldest and most genuine section of the race. Chlojo, or Clodio,[4] may be regarded as the earliest historic holder of the strictly royal authority, or the Hoard of the Nibelungen. The Franks had already victoriously invaded the Roman world and dwelt there under the name of Confederates in the former Roman Belgia. Clodio ruled a subject province with something like a proconsul's power. Very probably a decisive battle with Roman legions had preceded this final seizure, and in the spoil there may have been found, in addition to the war-chest, the full insignia of Roman empire. With these treasures, these insignia, the saga of the

4 See note 2 on p. 154.

Nibelungen Hoard would gain new realistic matter as further inspiration, and its ideal import would be renewed by the increase in the royal stability of the old ruling race. The previously divided royal authority was thus united, materially and spiritually, and the degenerate tribal system broke against it in vain. To the many collateral branches of the royal house the advantage of this new power would be equally obvious, and they persistently strove to grasp it for themselves. Such an immediate kinsman was Merovech, chieftain of the Merwegau, to whose protection the dying Clodio gave his three infant sons. Instead of parcelling out their birthright to his charges, the faithless cousin seized it for himself and drove the helpless children out. This trait we also meet in the fully-fledged Nibelungen saga, where Siegfried von Morungen, i.e. Merwungen, has to divide the heirloom Hoard among the sons of Nibelung, but likewise keeps it for himself. The power and right residing in the Hoard had thus passed over to the Nibelungen's blood relations, the Merwingen. In effect, they added to its wealth by constant conquest and enlargement of the royal might, achieving the latter by a systematic destruction of all the blood-relations of their house.

One of the sons of Clodio, however, was saved. His descendants fled to Austrasia, regained the Nibelgau, established themselves at Nivella, and finally reappeared in history as the 'Pipingen', a name unquestionably given them by the hearty sympathy of the people for the fate of those little sons of Clodio, and accepted in due gratitude for this people's helping and protecting love. This dynasty, after recovery of the Nibelungen Hoard, increased the extent of the worldly power bestowed by it. Charlemagne, whose predecessor had finally entirely set aside the puffed-up and degenerate race of the Merwingen, gained and governed the whole German world, together with the former West-Roman Empire in so far as German peoples dwelt therein. He accordingly considered himself *de facto* successor to the rights of the Roman Caesars, and claimed their confirmation by the Pope.

At this point, we must now survey the state of the world at that time, from the viewpoint of the mighty Nibelung himself; for this is the moment in history which gives us the clearest idea of the great Frankish saga.

When Charlemagne looked down from the height of his West-Roman Emperor's throne upon the world he knew, the first thing to strike him must have been that solely in himself and his family had the ancient German kingship survived. All the royal races of the German peoples that had been related to him, so far as language proved a common origin, had passed away or been destroyed by subjugation, and he could thus consider himself the only representative and lawful heir of the old German king-hood. This state of affairs would very naturally lead him and his nearest kin, the Franks, to regard themselves as peculiarly privileged, as the oldest and most imperishable dynasty of the whole German nation, and eventually to find an ideal right to that pretension in their primitive family chronicles. In those chronicles, as in similar primeval sagas, an originally religious core is plainly visible. Though we left that idea on one side before, we should now view it more closely.

ORIGIN AND EVOLUTION OF THE NIBELUNGEN MYTH

Man receives his first impressions from surrounding nature, and none of her phenomena will have reacted on him more forcibly from the beginning, than that which seemed to him to form the first condition of existence, or at least of his knowledge of everything contained in creation: light and day and the sun. Gratitude, and finally worship, would be accorded this element above all; the more so, as its opposite, darkness, or night, seemed joyless, hence unfriendly and fear-compelling. Now, as man drew all his joy and animation from the light, it would soon come to signify the very fount of his being: it became the be-getter, the father, the god. The breaking of day out of night at last appeared to him the victory of light over darkness, of warmth over cold, and so forth. This idea may have been the first to breed in man a moral consciousness and to lead him to distinguish between the useful and the harmful, the friendly and hostile, the good and the bad.

So far, at any rate, this earliest nature-impression must be regarded as the common basis of the religions of all races. The formulation of these general ideas derived from physical observation, however, led in due course to the various religions differing according to the character of different nations. Now the race saga of the Franks has the high pre-eminence that, in keeping with the race's special position, it developed more and more from this beginning to historical significance, whereas a similar growth of the religious myth into genealogical saga is nowhere to be found among the other German races. In exact degree as these lagged behind in influencing history, their race-sagas stop short at the religious myth (this is superlatively the case with the Scandinavians), or get lost in wholly undeveloped fragments at the first point of contact with more active historic nations.

At the farthest point to which we can trace them, the Frankish chronicles involved the personified Light- or Sun-god, who conquers and lays low the monster of ancient chaotic night. This is the original meaning of Siegfried's fight with the Dragon, a fight like that which Apollo fought against the dragon Python. Yet, as day succumbs to night again, as summer in the end must yield to winter, Siegfried too is slain at last. So the god became man, and as a mortal man he fills our soul with fresh and stronger sympathy. For, a sacrifice to his deed of blessing us, he wakes the moral motive of revenge, the longing to avenge his death upon his murderer, and thus renew his deed. The ancient fight is now continued by ourselves, and its issue is similar to that eternal alternation of day and night, summer and winter, and lastly of the human race itself, in ceaseless sway from life to death, from triumph to defeat, from joy to grief, and thus perennially rejuvenating in itself the active consciousness of the immortal role of man and nature. The quintessence of this constant expression of life was finally personified in Wotan

(Zeus) as the chief god, the father and pervader of all things. Though he was by nature the highest god, and as such had to assume the role of father to the other deities, yet he was not an historically older god, but sprang into existence from man's later, higher consciousness of self. Consequently he is more abstract than the older nature god, whilst the latter is more corporeal and, so to speak, more personally inborn in man.

If this may pass as a general statement of the evolutionary path of the chronicles and finally of history, from the ancient myth, our next concern will be with that part of the Franks' chronicle which gave this race its quite specific physiognomy, to wit, the *Hoard.*

In the religious myths of the Scandinavians, the term *Nifelheim,* i.e. Nibel or Nebelheim (the Home of Mists) comes down to us as a designation of the subterranean region of the Night-spirits, 'Schwarzalben', as opposed to the heavenly dwelling of the 'Asen' and 'Lichtalben' (Light-elves). These Black-elves, 'Niflûngar', children of night and death, burrow in the earth, find out its inner treasures, smelt and smith its ore. Golden gear and keen-edged weapons are their work. Now we find the names of the Nibelungen, their treasures, arms and trinkets, again in the Frankish chronicles, but with the distinction that the idea originally shared by all the German races here takes on historic ethic significance.

When light vanquished darkness, when Siegfried slew the Nibelungen dragon, he won as further victor's spoil the Nibelungen Hoard it guarded. But the possession of this Hoard, whose properties increased his might beyond all measure, since he thereby rules the Nibelungen, is also the cause of his death; for the dragon's heir now plots to win it back. This heir despatches him by stealth, as night the day, and drags him down into the gloomy realm of death: Siegfried thus becomes himself a Nibelung. Though doomed to death by acquisition of the Hoard, each subsequent generation strives to seize it. Its inmost essence drives it on, as with a law of Nature, as day has ever to dethrone the night anew. For in the Hoard there lies the secret of all earthly might: it is the earth itself with all its splendour, which in the joyful shining of the sun at dawn we recognise as our possession to enjoy, when night, that spread its ghostly, gloomy dragon's-wings fearsomely above the world's rich realm, has finally been routed.

If we look more closely at this Hoard, the Nibelungen's special work, we recognise firstly the mineral wealth of the earth, and secondly man's use of this: arms, the ruler's regalia and stores of gold. So that Hoard included in itself the means of gaining and insuring mastery, and was also the one talisman of the ruler. The hero-god who won it first, and thus became a Nibelung partly through his power and partly through his death, left as heirloom to his race the active right to claim the Hoard. To avenge the slain and keep or win the Hoard afresh, is the task required by the spirit of the race. This fate distinguishes the race of the Nibelungen-Franken throughout its saga and above all in its history.

Now, if it is thought too daring to assume that even in the ancient home of the German tribes that wondrous race once reigned above them all, or, if the other German stems have sprung from it, that it once ruled at the head of all other peoples on that Asiatic mountain-isle, at least a later phase is irrefutable: that it actually governed all the German races in Europe, and at their head, as we soon shall see, both claimed and strove for the dominion of every nation in the world. That deep inner urge, at times stronger than at others, this race of kings appears to have ascribed in every age to its prime origin. Charlemagne knew perfectly what he was doing, and why, when he had all the songs of the old sagas most carefully collected and transcribed: he knew they would confirm the people's belief in the age-old right of his dynasty.

THE RANK OF ROMAN EMPEROR AND THE
ROMAN RACE SAGA

The ruling instinct of the Nibelungen, till then brutal in its satisfaction, was led at last by Charlemagne towards an ideal aim : this psychological change was brought about by Charlemagne's assumption of the *Roman Caesardom*.

If we cast a glance at the world outside the German lands as Charlemagne knew it, we find the selfsame kingless plight as with the subject German races. The Romanised nations ruled by him had long since lost their royal dynasties under Roman domination; the Slavonic nations, little valued in themselves and destined for a more or less thorough Germanising, had never won for their ruling races, now also falling to decay, a recognition equal to the German's. Rome alone retained her historic claim to rule the world; and although world-dominion had been exerted by the Caesars in the name of a people, not of an ancient royal race, it was nevertheless in the form of a monarchy. These Caesars, in latter days capriciously selected first from this, then that component of the mixture of nations, had never been required to prove a racial right to the highest sovereignty in all the world. The deep corruption, impotence, and shameful foundering of this Roman Caesarate, propped up at last by nothing but the German mercenaries, who had possession of the Roman Empire long before its actual extinction, had certainly not faded from the memory of its Frankish conquerors. Yet, for all the personal weakness and depravity of the emperors known to the Germans, a deep awe and reverence of that rank under whose authority this highly-cultured Roman world was ruled had been implanted in the minds of the barbaric intruders, and had remained there until these later times. And in that feeling there probably lurked, not only respect for a higher culture, but also an old remembrance of the first brush of the German peoples with the Romans, who

under Julius Caesar had once reared a strong and lasting dam
against their restless inroads.

German warriors had hunted Gauls and Celts, who offered
little resistance, over the Alps and across the Rhine. The conquest
of the whole of Gaul was easily within their grasp, when suddenly they encountered in Julius Caesar a force previously unknown to them. Beating them back, vanquishing and partly
subjugating them, this extraordinary soldier must have made an
indelible impression on the Germans. Their deep awe of him
was confirmed when they later learnt how all the Roman world
had bent to him, how his patronymic 'Caesar' had been hallowed
to the title of the highest earthly might, whilst he himself had
been translated to the gods from whom his race had sprung.

This divine descent was grounded on an ancient Roman saga,
according to which the Romans issued from a primordial race
that, originally coming from Asia, had settled on the banks of
the Tiber and the Arno. The religious obeisance offered to the
offspring of this race was, for centuries, indisputably the most
important heritage of the Roman nation : in it reposed the force
that bound and knit this active people together. The 'sacra' in
the keeping of the oldest, immemorially-allied patrician families,
compelled the heterogeneous masses of plebeians to obedience.
Deep awe and veneration of the holy objects, whose presence
enjoined a vigorous abstemiousness (as practised by the sorely-
tried father of the race), gave rise to the oldest, most effective
laws whereby the headstrong plebeians were governed; and the
pontifex maximus, as each one succeeded Numa, the moral
founder of the Roman State, was the virtual spiritual king of the
Romans. Actual kings, or hereditary holders of the highest
worldly rulership, are unknown in Roman history. The banished
Tarquins were Etruscan conquerors; in their expulsion we have
to recognise not so much a political act of insurrection against
the royal power as the old national act of shaking off a foreign
yoke.

Now, when the plebeian element was no longer to be held in
check by these stern and spiritually-armoured ancient races;

when through constant warfare and privation it had made its strength so irresistible that, to prevent it being let loose against the State itself, it must be loosed upon the outer world, then, and still more as a result of its conquests, the last bond with the ancient customs slowly snapped. Dominion over the world, enslavement of its peoples, and not dominion over the inner man and control of his egoistic animal passions, was henceforth Rome's religion. The Pontificate, though it still stood as outward token of the ancient Rome, passed over to the worldly Imperator as his weightiest attribute. The first man to combine both powers was Julius Caesar, whose race was lauded as the very oldest to emerge from Asia. Troja, so said the old chronicle now grown to historic consciousness, was that sacred town of Asia whence the Julian race had sprung. During the destruction of his birthplace by the united Hellenic tribes, Aeneas, son of a goddess, had rescued the holiest relic (the Palladium)[5] preserved in this primeval people's city, and brought it safe to Italy. From him descend the primal Roman races, and most directly of them all the Julian. From him, too, through the possession of that holy relic, was said to spring the core of ancient Rome, its religion.

TROJAN DESCENT OF THE FRANKS

How significant is the historically attested fact that, shortly after the foundation of their rule in Roman Gaul, the Franks announced that they were likewise descended from the Trojan dynasty. The historian gives a pitying smile at such an absurd idea, which surely cannot hold a grain of truth. But he whose purpose is to vindicate the deeds of men and races by their inmost views and impulses, will find it most important to note what they believed, or tried to make others believe, about themselves. And no feature can be of more striking historic importance,

[5] The wooden statue of Pallas Athene in the city of Troy. It was said to have fallen from heaven, and it was believed that as long as it remained within the city, Troy would be safe.

than this naïve statement of the Franks' belief in their ancient
right to rule, upon their entry into that Roman world whose
culture and whose past inspired them with reverence, and the
right to rule which they proudly based directly on the principles
of the classical Roman world itself. So they, too, sprang from
Troy; in fact it was their royal race that once governed in Troy.
For one of their ancient kings, Pharamond, was none other than
Priam, the very head of the Trojan royal family, who after the
destruction of the city, so they said, had journeyed into distant
parts with a remnant of his people. The first point for us to
notice here, is that the naming of towns or transformation of
their names by an addendum, as also the poetic adaptations of
the Trojan War and allied incidents in vogue until the later
Middle Ages, afford sufficient evidence of the widespread and
lasting influence of the new saga. Whether it was in all respects
as new as it appears, or if it contained a germ far older than its
new disguise in this Graeco-Roman dress suggests, is certainly
worth looking into.

The myth of an ancient town or castle, built by the earliest
human races and circled with Cyclopean walls to guard their
holiest fetish, we find in the legends of almost every nation of the
world, especially of those which we may assume spread westwards
from the primeval hills of Asia. Did not the archetype of these
fabled cities actually once exist in these peoples' earliest home?
Surely there was one original walled city, which held in it the
oldest and most venerable race, the source of all patriarchism,
that is, of knighthood joined with priesthood. The farther the
races migrated westward from their ancient home, the holier
would their memory of that primordial city grow. It became to
them a city of the gods, the Asgard of the Scandinavians, the
Asciburg of the related Germans. On the Greek Olympos we find
again this dwelling-place of the gods, and the gods may have
hovered, too, above the Roman Capitol. This much is certain,
that wherever the races, now grown to nations, made their home,
there that legendary town was copied. The sanctity of the primordial city was gradually transferred to the new national capital

of the oldest ruling dynasty of kings and priests; and the farther the races journeyed from this new city in its turn, to build afresh, the more brightly did the original glamour of the legend shine on their new capital. Very naturally, however, with the freer evolution of these racial communities, and their growing sense of self-reliance, the desire for independence tended to arise. This occurred when the ancient ruling race, that governed from the new capital city, endeavoured to imprint its sovereignty on the offshoot communities or cities, and met their stiffening resistance with added tyranny. The first national wars of independence were therefore those waged by colonies against the mother-cities; and so obstinate must have grown their enmity, that nothing less than the destruction of the ancient capital, with the extirpation or total banishment of the hereditary ruling race, could assuage the hate of the colonists or allay their fears of fresh oppression. All the great historic nations that followed in each other's foot-steps from the Indian Caucasus to the Mediterranean Sea had such a holy city, copied from the primeval city of the gods on earth, and saw its destruction by new generations. Very probably they even nursed the memory of an ancient war of the earliest races against the eldest ruling race in that abode of the gods, that town which was then destroyed. This may have been, in fact, the first battle for the Nibelung's Hoard.

We know nothing of any great mother-cities founded by our German races on the model of the ancient town in their long north-westward wanderings, which finally came to an end at the German Ocean and were stopped by the sword of Julius Caesar. On the other hand, the memory of the city of the gods in their original homeland had lingered with them, and although it had no earthly form, it had been transformed into the more abstract notion of an abode of the gods in Asgard. Not until they came to their new and more stable home, in our present Germany, do we find any signs of Asenburgs.

The evolution of the peoples thrusting south-westwards had been quite different. Among the Hellenic races, the last distinct remembrance of their united fight for independence against the

Priamids, and the razing of Troy which represented the beginning
of a new historic life, had almost totally extinguished every other
memory. Now, just as the Romans in their turn, after a closer
acquaintance with the historic chronicle of the Hellenes, felt
completely justified in assuming a link between the dim remem-
brances of their forefathers' coming from Asia and that clear-cut
myth of the more highly cultured nation (as if by thus subjugating
the Greeks to their purpose they could make reprisals for the
destruction of Troy), so the Franks seized on this myth also,
perhaps with no less justification, when they came to know the
legend and its sequel. If the German memories were less distinct,
at least they were even older, for they clung directly to the earliest
home, the burg (Etzel- or Asci-burg) in which the Nibelungen
Hoard was stored and from which it was once won by their
national God and bequeathed to them, the burg whence they
had once already ruled all kindred folks and races. The Grecian
Troy became for them that mother-city; and the king of im-
memorial right, dislodged therefrom, revived his ancient privilege
in them.

Confronted with the history of the wanderers to the south-west,
must not this race regard its wondrous preservation as a token
of the gods' eternal preference? All peoples now descended from
the races that had waged a patricidal war against the oldest royal
race in their original home, and, victorious, had forced this race
to journey towards the raw inhospitable north while they moved
to the fertile south in leisurely expansion, all these the Franks
found kingless. The oldest ruling tribes were long since extinct.
A last Greek king, the Macedonian Alexander, offspring of
Achilles, that foremost vanquisher of Troy, had been Lord over
the whole southern Orient, up to the cradle of mankind in central
Asia, as if in a last enactment of that earliest patricidal war. With
him his race expired also, and from that time the only rulers
were unlawful usurpers of the royal power, who all finally suc-
cumbed beneath the weight of Julian Rome.

After the extinction of the Julian race even the Roman
emperors were arbitrarily elected, and certainly not racially

legitimate, dictators. Their empire, before they themselves became aware of it, had long since ceased to be a 'Roman' empire. From of old it had only been held together by military force and, now that the Roman nations were completely degenerate and effeminate, these armies were formed almost entirely of hired troops of German origin. Thus, gradually renouncing all material worldly might, after long estrangement from itself the Roman spirit turned back to its original nature. Adopting Christianity, it gave birth to a new development, the Roman Catholic Church: the Imperator again became all Pontifex, Caesar again Numa, but with a new significance. Now the *Pontifex maximus,* or Pope, was approached by the representative of ancient imperial might, Charlemagne. The bearers of the oldest kinghood and the oldest priesthood, split since the razing of the cradle city (according to the Trojan saga these were the royal Priam and the pious Aeneas) met together once more after centuries of parting, to represent the body and spirit of mankind.

Their meeting was a joyful one: nothing would ever part them again. One would give the other friendship and shelter. The Pontifex crowned the Caesar, and preached that the nations should obey their lawful king; the Emperor installed the Priest of God in his supreme pastorate, and undertook to shield him with the arm of worldly strength against all evil-doers.

Now, if the king was *de facto* master of the West-Roman empire, and if the thought of the old kingly title of his race was likely to awake in him the claim to perfect sovereignty of the world, with the title of emperor he assumed still stronger rights to that claim, especially as he was entrusted to protect that Christian Church which was to span the world. For the further development of that majestic world-empire, however, it is most important to note that this spiritual title did not set up a novel claim of the Frankish royal race, but simply revealed in plainer terms a claim implicit in the germ of the Frankish saga, though it had been veiled till then in the dimmer recesses of consciousness.

MATERIAL AND IDEAL CONTENTS OF THE NIBELUNGEN HOARD

With Charlemagne, the oft-cited ancient myth attains its most material manifestation in a grand harmonious moment of world history. Thenceforward, as its outward embodiment dissolved and fell to pieces, its essential ideal content was to rise to such a pitch that, entirely divested of the real, the ideal was consummated by history, and finally withdrew into the realm of myth once more.

In the century after Charlemagne, under his increasingly incompetent successors, the actual kingdom and sovereignty over subject peoples crumbled away and lost its power, but the cruelty of the Carlovingians remained, and this sprang from one instinct common to them all, the longing for sole possession of the Nibelungen Hoard, of the power to rule supreme. After Charlemagne, this seemed to need confirmation through the emperorship, and he who won the emperor's throne believed himself the true possessor of the Hoard, whatever the diminution of his worldly wealth (in landed property). The emperorship, with the supreme authority attaching to it alone, was thus invested with an increasingly symbolic aura, and during the period of the total defeat of the Frankish ruling dynasty, when the Saxon Otto appeared to be restoring the real Caesarate of Charlemagne in a fresh recreation of Rome, its ideal aspect moved towards ever clearer consciousness in the mind of that ancient dynasty. The Franks and their ducal race of Carlovingian blood, with the saga in mind, may have said to themselves something like this : 'Even though the real possession of the land is torn from us, and once more we are thrown upon ourselves, if we can regain the imperial rank, for which we shall never cease to strive, we will again win our ancient title to mastery of the world. Then we shall know how to use it better than these usurpers of the Hoard, who do not even understand it.'

In effect, as soon as the Frankish race regained power, the question of worldly power became increasingly important, mainly owing to the relationship between State and Church.

In proportion as the worldly power lost much of its real estate and approached a more spiritual development, the originally idealistic Church acquired more worldly possessions. Each party seemed to realise that, for its secure establishment, it must assimilate what it had at first lacked. From both sides, therefore, the original antithesis built up to an open fight for the prize at stake, exclusive world-dominion. Because of the growing consciousness of both parties in this increasingly stubborn fight, the Emperor was at last forced to see the necessity of acquiring the spiritual dominion of the world, if he wanted to safeguard his earthly title. The Pope, on the other hand, would have to annihilate these worldly claims, or rather take them to himself, if he meant to remain or become the actual governor and overseer of the World Church.

The resultant demands of the Pope were grounded upon Christian reason in the sense that he felt bound to defend the Spirit's supremacy over the Flesh. The Emperor, on the contrary, saw that his prime concern was to prove his power and claims to be quite independent of any hallowing or ratifying, to say nothing of bestowal, by the Pope. For this purpose he found what he deemed a perfect title in the ancient belief of his race and its origin.

In its earliest form, the chronicle of the Nibelungen went back to the memory of a primordial father, not only of the Franks, but perhaps of all those nations which had issued from the Asiatic home. Very naturally, as we find with every patriarchal system, the royal and priestly powers had been combined in one and the same person. The later division of these powers would be a consequence of a dissension in the race, or, had the priestly power devolved on all the fathers of the commune, it could be recognised in them, but never in an upstart priest opposed to the king. The fulfilment of the priestly office, in so far as it was to be assigned to one individual, could fall to no one but the king, as father of the people. That there was no need for those notions to be sacrificed *in toto* on the conversion to Christianity, is proved by the facts, and may be deduced with little trouble from the essential content of the old traditions. The abstract highest god of the Germans, Wuotan, did not really need to yield place to the God of the Christians; he could be completely identified with him. It was merely the physical trappings with which the various races had clothed him in accordance with their idiosyncrasy, their dwelling-place and climate, that were to be stripped off. The universal attributes ascribed to him, completely corresponded to those allotted to the Christian's God. And Christianity has been unable to this day to extirpate the elemental or local nature gods : quite recent legends and a wealth of current superstitions, attest this today in our nineteenth century.

But that one original god, from whom all races derived their earthly being, was certainly the last to be given up : for in him was found a striking likeness to Christ himself, the Son of God. He too died, was mourned and avenged, as we still avenge Christ on the Jews of today. Fidelity and attachment were transferred to Christ all the more easily, because the original god was seen in Him once more, and if Christ, as Son of God, was father (at least in a spiritual sense) of *all* men, that harmonised still further with the idea of the divine primordial father of the Franks, who considered themselves the oldest race and parent of all others. Christianity therefore, because of their incomplete and physical understanding of it, tended rather to strengthen the Franks in their national faith, particularly against the Roman Church, than to make them falter. In reply to this vital obstinacy of the Wibelingian superstition, we see the natural instinct of the Church to attack with an almost deadly fervour this last and sturdiest survival of paganism in the deeply hated race.

THE 'GHIBELLINE' EMPIRE AND FREDERICK I

It is highly significant that the urge towards ideal vindication of their claims becomes more pronounced in the Wibelingen or Wibelungen (to give them their historic folk-name) in proportion as their line departs from immediate kinship with the primeval ruling race. If in Charlemagne this blood kinship was still at the height of its ancestral strength, in the Hohenstaufian Frederick I we see almost nothing but an idealised kinship. The imperial role could be justified less and less by blood ties or material wealth, and became an idealised concept.

Under the last two emperors of the Frankish ducal race of the Salier, the great fight with the Church had begun in deadly earnest. Henry V, previously supported by the Church against his hapless father, had scarcely reached the rank of emperor when he felt the fateful craving to renew his father's struggle with the Church, and, as if it were the only means of combating her claims, to extend his dominion over her as well. He must have divined that the emperor would be powerless if his world-dominion did not include dominion of the Church herself. It is characteristic, on the other hand, that the interim non-Wibeling-ian Emperor Lothair adopted an attitude of peaceful submission to the Church. He did not understand what his rank implied; *his* claims did not extend to the world-dominion; that was the inheritance of the Wibelingen, the old legitimist contenders for the Hoard. But, more clearly and plainly than his ancestors, Frederick I took up his inheritance in its sublimest sense. The whole inner and outer depravity of the world appeared to him the necessary consequence of the weakness and incompleteness with which the Emperor's power had been exerted thitherto. The material condition of his realm, already in decline, had to be maintained and improved by the emperor's authority; and that could only be enhanced when its extreme pretensions were enforced. Frederick the Great's vision might be summarised, in the colloquial speech of today, somewhat as follows:

'In the German people there survives the oldest lawful race of kings in the whole world. This race issues from a son of God, called *Christ* by the remaining nations of the earth. For the welfare of his race, and the peoples of the earth derived therefrom, he wrought a most glorious deed, and for that deed's sake he suffered death. The nearest heirs of his great deed, and of the power won thereby, are the "Nibelungen", to whom the earth belongs for the happiness of every nation. The Germans are the oldest nation, their king is a "Nibelung", and at their head he claims world-rulership. There can therefore exist no right to any sort of possession or enjoyment, in the whole world, that does not emanate from him and require its hallowing by his sanction. All property not bestowed or sanctioned by the Emperor is illegal, and counts as stolen, for the Emperor sanctions for the good, possession or enjoyment, of *all*, whereas the individual's gain is for itself and stolen from all. The Emperor grants these things to the Germans himself; all other nations must receive confirmation from their kings and princes as attorneys of the Emperor, from whom all earthly sovereignty originally flows, as the planets and their moons receive their radiance from the sun. Thus too the Emperor delegates the high-priestly power, originally no less pertaining to him than the earthly might, to the Pope of Rome: the latter has to exercise the Will of God in his name, and to acquaint him with God's decree, that he may execute the Heavenly Will in the name of God upon the earth. The Pope is accordingly the Emperor's most important officer, and because of this it is all the more essential that the Emperor keeps a strict watch that the Pope uses his delegated power for the peace and healing of all nations upon earth.'

It is on this level that we must assess Frederick's estimate of his supreme rank, his divine right, if we are to judge correctly the motives for his actions.

We see him in the first place securing his worldly power by settling internal strife through a reconciliation with his relatives the Welfen, and compelling the princes of bordering peoples, in particular the Danes, Poles and Hungarians, to accept their lands in fee from him. Thus fortified he fared to Italy, and, as arbiter over the Lombards in the Roncalian Diet, for the first time published to the world a systematic digest of the Emperor's claims, in which, for all the influence of Imperial Roman principles, we recognise the strictest consequences of the aforesaid view of his authority : his imperial right was here extended even to the granting of air and water.

No less determined were his claims against and over the Church herself, after an initial period of reserve. A disputed Papal election gave him the opportunity of exerting his supreme right. With strict observance of what he deemed fit priestly etiquette, he had the election scrutinised, deposed the Pope who seemed to him at fault, and installed the vindicated rival in his place.

Every trait of Frederick's every undertaking, each decree, bears indisputable witness to the energy with which he strove to realise his high ideal. The unwavering firmness with which he opposed the no less obstinate Pope Alexander III, the almost superhuman rigour, in an emperor by no means prone to cruelty by nature, with which he strove to overthrow the equally un-daunted Milan, are evidence of the grand idea which moved him.

Two mighty foes, however, stood up against the imperious world-king : the first at the starting-point of his material power, in the German landed system, and the second at the terminus of his ideal endeavour, the Catholic Church established in the conscience of Romanic peoples in particular. Both foes joined forces with a third, which the Emperor, in a sense, had himself first brought to consciousness : the instinct for freedom in the Lombard communes.

If the earliest resistance of the German races had had its origin in their thirst for freedom from their Frankish rulers, that wish had gradually passed over from the shattered tribal fellowships to the lords. Although the efforts of these princes had all the evil attributes of selfish lust, yet their longing for independence might rank in their eyes as a fight for freedom, however less exalted it must seem to us. The Church's impulse towards freedom was more ideal by far, and more universal. In Christian terminology it could be seen as the struggle of the soul for liberation from the fetters of the sensual world, and undoubtedly it passed for such in the minds of the greatest princes of the Church. Christianity had been forced to share too deeply in the world's material taste for might, however, and her ultimate victory could therefore be gained only by the ruin of her inmost soul.

But the spirit of freedom shines out most purely in the Lombard townships, and precisely (alas! almost solely) in their decisive fights with Frederick. These fights are the most remarkable event of a critical historical period, as it is in them, for the first time in the history of the world, that the spirit of original human freedom embodied in the burgher commune prepared itself for a struggle to the death with an old established, all-embracing sovereignty. Athens' fight against the Persians was patriotic opposition to a huge monarchic piracy: all similar famous deeds of single townships, until the time of the Lombards, bear the selfsame character of defence of an ancient racial independence against a foreign conqueror. Now, this freedom, defended by a nation until then untroubled, was never present with the Lombard communes. History has seen the population of these cities, compounded of all nations and without any old traditions, fall shameful victim to the greed of conqueror after conqueror. Through a thousand years of total impotence, no nation lived in these cities, that is no race with any consciousness of its earliest origins. In them were merely men, men led by the need to insure an undisturbed mutual prosperity to an ever plainer evolution of the principles of society, and their realisation through the community.

These novel principles, devoid of any racial lore or myth arising purely of and for itself, owe their historic origin to the population of the Lombard cities, who, imperfectly as they could understand and turn these principles to a lasting good, nevertheless managed to evolve from their lowly condition to become agents of the highest calibre. If the entry of Lombardy into history is to count as the spark that leaps from the stone, then Frederick is the steel that struck it from the stone.

Frederick, the representative of the last ancient racial kinghood, in the mightiest fulfilment of his inevitable destiny, struck from the stone of manhood the spark before whose splendour he himself had to pale. The Pope launched his ban, the Welf Henry forsook his king in his direst need, but the sword of the Lombard band of brothers smote the imperial warrior at the terrible rout at Legnano.[6]

TRANSFORMATION OF THE IDEAL CONTENT OF THE HOARD INTO THE 'HOLY GRAIL'

The world-ruler recognised from whence his deepest wound had come, and who it was that cried a halt to his world-plan. It was the spirit of free manhood loosed from the trammels of race, that had faced him in this Lombard bond. He made short work of both the older foes : to the high priest he gave his hand, and he fell with crushing force upon the selfish Guelphs. So, once more arrived at the summit of his power and undisputed might, he freed the Lombards, and made a lasting peace with them.

At Mainz he gathered his whole empire round him. He wished to greet all his vassals, from the first to the last, once more. The clergy and the laity surrounded him; from every land kings sent ambassadors with precious gifts, in homage to his imperial might. Then Palestine sent forth to him a cry to save the Holy Tomb. Frederick turned his gaze to the land of morning. An irresistible force drew him on towards Asia, to the cradle of the nations, to the place where God begat the father of all men. He had heard wonderful legends of a lordly country deep in Asia, in farthest India, of a primeval divine priest-king who governed a pure and happy people there, who were immortal because of

[6] Frederick made a definitive peace with the Lombard League at Constance in June 1183.

a miraculous relic called the Holy Grail. Might he there regain the lost image of God, now garbled by ambitious priests in Rome according to their pleasure?

The old hero set forth. With a splendid military retinue he marched through Greece: he could have conquered it but preferred to forge ahead to farthest Asia. There, in tempestuous battle, he broke the power of the Saracens. The promised land lay unchallenged before him. He could not wait for the construction of a flying bridge, but forged impatiently eastwards. He plunged into the stream on horseback: no one saw him alive again. Since then, the legend has been told that once the Keeper of the Grail had really brought the holy relic to the West. He had performed great wonders, but, in the Netherlands, the Nibelungen's ancient seat, a Knight of the Grail had appeared, and vanished again when asked forbidden tidings of his origin. Then the Grail was conducted back by its former guardian to the distant Orient. In a castle on a remote mountain in India it was now kept once more.

In truth the legend of the Holy Grail, significantly enough, first occurs at the very time when the empire attained a more spiritual impulse, and the Nibelung's Hoard was accordingly losing its material significance, which was replaced by a greater spiritual content. The spiritual transmutation of the Hoard into the Grail was accomplished in the German conscience: and the Grail, at least in the meaning lent it by German poets, must rank as the ideal representation or follower of the Nibelungen Hoard. It, too, had sprung from Asia, from the primeval home of mankind. God had guided it to men as a paragon of holiness.

It is of the greatest importance that its Keeper should be priest and king alike, that is, a master of all spiritual knighthood, such as has been introduced from the Orient in the twelfth century. So this master was in truth none other than the Emperor, from whom all chivalry proceeded. Thus the real and ideal world-supremacy, the union of the highest kinghood and priesthood, seemed completely personified by the Emperor.

The quest of the Grail henceforth replaces the struggle for the Nibelungen Hoard; and, as the occidental world, unsatisfied

spiritually, reached out past Rome and Pope to find its source
of healing in the tomb of the Redeemer at Jerusalem, as, unsatisfied even there, it cast its yearning gaze, half spiritual, half
physical, still farther toward the East to find the primal shrine of
manhood, so the Grail was said to have withdrawn from our
ribald West to the pure, chaste, unattainable birthplace of all
nations.

To review the ancient Nibelungen saga once more, we see it
springing like a spiritual seed from the primeval race's earliest
view of nature. We see this seed develop to a mighty plant on
ever more material soil, especially in the historic evolution of
the saga, so that in Charlemagne it seems to thrust its knotty
fibres deep into the actual earth. Finally, in the Wibelingian
empire of Frederick I, we see this plant unfold its fairest flower
to the light. With him the flower faded. With his grandson
Frederick II, the most high-minded of all these emperors, the
wondrous perfume of the dying bloom spread like a lovely magic
spell through the entire world of west and east, until with the
grandson of the last-named emperor, the youthful Conradin, the
leafless withered stem was torn with all its roots and fibres from
the ground, and stamped to dust.

HISTORIC RESIDUE OF THE MATERIAL CONTENT OF THE HOARD, IN 'PROPERTY'

A shriek of horror rang through every country when the head
of Conradin fell in Naples at the command of Charles d'Anjou,[7]
who presents the perfect archetype of all post-Wibelingian kinghood. He sprang from the oldest of the newer royal races, the
French Capets, and succeeded the last French Carlovingian.
Hugo Capet's origin was well known. Everybody knew what his

---

[7] Conradin was defeated by Charles at Tagliacozzo on 23rd August, 1268.
He was taken prisoner, tried as a rebel and executed at Naples.

race had once been, and how he arrived at the throne. Cunning, policy, and even violence were his tools and those of his successors, compounding for the right they lacked in the people's eyes. These Capets, in all their later branches, were the pattern for the modern king- and prince-hood. It could not seek foundation for its claims in any belief in racial descent. The world well knew by what means, usually violent ones, princes both attained to power and contrived to keep it.

With the foundering of the Wibelungen, mankind had been torn from the last thread whereby it still hung, in a sense, to its racial natural origin. The Hoard of the Nibelungen had evaporated to the realm of poetry and ideas. Only an earthly precipitate, property, remained as its dregs.

In the Nibelungen myth we found expressed by all the generations who devised, developed and enacted it, an uncommonly clear idea of the nature of property, of ownership. If in the oldest religious view the Hoard appeared to be the splendour of the earth laid bare to all by daylight, we later see it take on more solid form as the hero's booty, won from an odious adversary as the reward for the bravest, most astounding deed. This Hoard, this talisman of might, it is true, is henceforth claimed as a hereditary right by the descendants of that godlike hero; yet it has this characteristic, that it is never gained by lazy peace, by simple contract, but only through a deed akin to that of its first winner. Moreover, this constantly repeated deed of the heir has all the moral meaning of vendetta, of retribution for the murder of a kinsman. We see blood, passion, love, hate, in short, both physically and spiritually, purely human springs and motives at work in the winning of the Hoard; man restless and suffering, man doomed to conscious death by his own deed, his victory, and most of all by his possession, at the head of all things, of the roots of power. These views, which honoured man as the focus of all power, entirely corresponded with the mode of treating property in actual life. If in earliest antiquity there certainly prevailed the simplest and most natural principle of all, namely that the measure of possession or enjoyment must relate to man's need, among conquering nations with excess of goods the strength and prowess of the most renowned fighters naturally became the standard by which the richer spoils would be divided. In the historic feudal system, so long as it retained its pristine purity, we see this heroic-human principle still plainly voiced. The grant of a fief was merely to this one human being who had earned the right to claim reward for some decisive deed, some weighty service. From the moment when a fief became hereditary, the man, his personal excellence, his acts and deeds, lost value, which passed over to his property. Hereditary possession, no longer personal virtue, now gave their standing to his heirs, and the resulting deeper and deeper depreciation of man, against the higher and higher appreciation of property, was at last personified in the most inhuman institutions, such as those of primogeniture, from which, in strange perversity, the later nobility drew all their conceit and arrogance, without reflecting that by deriving their worth from a family possession they were openly disowning any actual human nobility.

So, after the fall of the heroic-human Wibelungen, this hereditary ownership, then property in general, possessions, became the title for all rights existing or to be acquired. Property gave man that right which man had theretofore conveyed to property. It was this dreg of the vanished Nibelungen Hoard, then, that the sobered German lords had kept: though the emperor might soar to the highest peak of the ideal, that which clung to the ground below, the duchies, palatinates, marks and counties, all ranks and offices granted by the emperor, were charged in the hands of his un-idealistic vassals utterly to mere possession, property. Possession was now consequently right. He who had a share in property, or managed to acquire one, from that instant ranked as a natural pillar of the State. What the most glorious emperors had claimed in good faith as their ideal title to rule the world, these practical gentry now applied to their possessions. The old divine right was arrogated to himself by every former crown-official; the God's-decree was expounded by Justinian's Roman Rights, and, to the bewilderment of property-enslaved mankind, transcribed in Latin law-books. Emperors were still appointed, though directly after the downfall of the Wibelungen their rank had already been hawked to the highest bidder. No sooner were they chosen, than they set to work to 'acquire' a goodly family seat 'by the grace of God', as one henceforth styled the forcible appropriation or nibbling-off of districts. Grown wiser, one gladly left domination of the world to the Christian God, who behaved far more leniently and humanely to the actually reigning selfish, depraved and vulgar sons of the Holy Roman Empire than the old heathen Nibelung warriors, who for any act of meanness made no bones about packing off a man from court and holding.

The peasant population sang, read, and in time printed the Nibelungenlieder, its only keepsake from the Hoard. Belief in it never wavered; but one knew it was no longer in the world, for it had been sunk into a mountain again, a cave like that whence Siegfried had once won it from the Nibelungen. The great Emperor himself had brought it back to that hill, to save it up for better times. There in the Kyffhäuser he sits, old Frederick Redbeard; all round him are the treasures of the Nibelungen, and by his side the sharp sword that once slew the dreaded dragon.

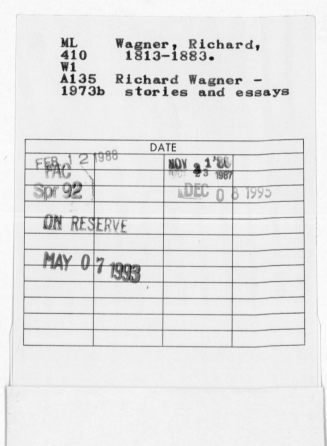